"This guide is easy to read ar... I feel energised and clear about what I want to change on my website and what needs my attention. I love Debbie's way of thinking about the audience and her tips on how to work with that effectively. Debbie explains the basics of website content and at no point do any of her suggestions feel overwhelming or unfathomable. I'm delighted to have this guide among my other copy-editing resources; I think it's a resource we should all have alongside our non-negotiable and steadfast references."

Alexis Grewan, Chairperson of the Professional Editors' Guild (PEG)

"This guide brings everything you need to know about making your editor website work hard for you into one place. The guide is extremely easy to follow and navigate thanks to Debbie's clear explanations, a good sprinkling of humour, and plenty of relevant real-life examples. It's also packed with helpful, actionable tips that you can implement straightaway. Definitely a must-read for any editor – whether your website is brand new or well established!"

Liz Pond, non-fiction editor and proofreader

"Debbie has created an invaluable resource for all of us editors. I already have a fairly decent website, but reading through this has reminded me that I should service it more often, and has also given me some great insight into things I have not yet done, or am maybe not optimising as well as I could. This is a resource I wish I had when I first began my journey; it would have made for a much clearer process. Truly a brilliant, informative, and valuable resource for both new and existing editors."

Jessica Runyard, copyeditor and proofreader

Improve Your Editor Website

A COMPREHENSIVE GUIDE

Debbie Emmitt

Improve Your Editor Website: A Comprehensive Guide
First Edition (2023)
First published by Stanbridge Press 2023
Copyright © 2023 Debbie Emmitt
All rights reserved

Legal notice

The fact that an organisation or website is referred to in this work as a citation and/or a potential source of further information does not mean that the author endorses the information the organisation or website may provide or recommendations it may make.

If you visit websites or pages referenced in this work, you do so at your own risk. The author is not liable and responsible for any damages which may arise from your actions in this regard.

ISBN: 978-1-7395107-1-8 (Hardcover)
ISBN: 978-1-7395107-0-1 (Paperback)

www.debbie-emmitt.com

Contents

Introduction

Why I wrote this book

Before becoming a full-time freelance editor and proofreader, I worked in the world of web content and marketing for 20 years. This book is the collision of those two worlds. It is my way of offering you, my fellow editor, all the web experience I have gathered during my 'previous life'.

As busy editors, we don't have much time to invest in getting our site up to scratch. It can be tempting to throw words and images down and not worry about how polished they look, whether the pages are search-engine friendly, or whether they're accessible to everyone regardless of device, platform or ability.

But this neglect is costing you potential clients.

When I was building my own website, I wanted to check I wasn't missing anything. I searched for a simple yet comprehensive guide that ran through every aspect to be considered by an editor looking to improve their site.

What I found was a minefield! Hundreds of results, none of which covered all the areas to work on. Even if you take the time to trawl through them, you'll find that many are over ten years old, which in web terms is the Stone Age.

There are lots of great resources for individual areas, or that list "top five ways to improve your site", but I couldn't find a one-stop shop containing every content angle you need to consider.

So, I wrote it myself.

What this guide is not about

Site setup

While I will be covering just about every element you need to consider when working on your editor webpages, I will not be explaining how to set up a site, the best platform on which to do this, or how to source a professional web designer.

There is a lot of information about this already available (a quick search engine foray will help you in this regard), and as platforms and processes can change quickly, this guide would go out of date in a flash.

Social media marketing

I will cover social media regarding how it directly relates to your website, but I will not go into detail about how to set up and maintain a social media campaign. If I did so, this guide would be twice the length, and you can find excellent advice on this area through a quick web search. Just check the date of the posts!

About me

I'm an editor, proofreader, mentor and author. I'm also a web content expert, having worked with websites for over 20 years. I began my career in the relatively early days of the web (2001), honing my skills on a multi-lingual, complex website affiliated with the University of Oxford, before going on to edit countless websites for other institutions.

I understand the importance of a professional, user-oriented website to raise awareness of your editing services, build your reputation and encourage potential clients to get in touch. I'm passionate about sharing my knowledge with fellow editors who don't have a background in web.

I can help you improve your website so it fulfils the needs of your visitors, adheres to contemporary best web practices and ultimately works as a powerful marketing tool for selling your services.

1 – Your Website Matters

Whether you're just starting out or are an established editor, a slick online presence is key.

Between 2005 and 2019, internet usage worldwide grew on average by 10% every year.[1]

While the rate of growth has since slightly slowed due to some parts of the world reaching saturation levels, in January 2023 there were still at least 1.9% more people using the internet than 12 months earlier.[2]

In 2022, 63.1% of the world's population was online (5.03 billion people),[2] with mobile internet accounting for over half of this.[3]

---

[1] 'Internet usage keeps growing, but barriers lie ahead', *Facts and Figures 2019 – Measuring Digital Development.* 2020 [Online]. Available: https://itu.foleon.com/itu/measuring-digital-development/internet-use [Accessed: 11 March 2023]

[2] Simon Kemp, *Digital 2023: Global Overview Report.* 2023 [Online]. Available: https://datareportal.com/reports/digital-2023-global-overview-report [Accessed: 11 March 2023]

[3] 'Percentage of mobile device website traffic worldwide from 1st quarter 2015 to 2nd quarter 2022'. *Statistica.* 2022 [Online]. Available: https://www.statista.com/statistics/277125/share-of-website-traffic-coming-from-mobile-devices/ [Accessed: 11 March 2023]

By establishing an online presence, you have an opportunity to connect with many more people than by any other marketing means.

Value of an editor website

If your site can be easily found by search engines, looks professional and is up to date, it will enable you to:

- **engage with potential clients**. Your target audience, whether authors, businesses, entrepreneurs, academics or other content producers, will find your site in search results. They will be impressed enough by your site to want to find out more about how you can help them.

- **have a central, accessible place** where your target clients and fellow editors can find out about you and your services, and to where any online reference to you can easily link (on social media, online directories, guest blogs, comments — absolutely anywhere online!).

- **own your corner of the internet.** It's best not to be totally reliant on third-party sites (social media, online directories, freelance job sites, etc.). If they are taken down, that marketing avenue disappears. You own your web domain.

Keep at it

Nothing is static in the online world. Facts about you and your services continually change. Images become dated. Web trends change, not only those concerning user behaviour and expectations, but browsers, platforms and devices constantly update too.

Your site needs frequent analysis and maintenance to remain up to date in terms of content, imagery and best web practice.

By working through this guide regularly (maybe each year), you can rest assured your site will always be in tip-top condition.

A helping hand

If applying all the knowledge in this guide seems daunting, help is at hand.

Mentoring

My editor mentoring service will offer you advice and support on improving your online editor presence. It is carefully tailored to your requirements, no matter your level of expertise.

I will shape the sessions around your needs and goals for our time together, whether minutes, weeks or months.

To find out more, visit **www.debbie-emmitt.com/mentoring-for-editors**

Web content services

I also offer two web content services – web text editing and website proofreading – to help you polish your web content and spot errors on your website.

Find out more at **www.debbie-emmitt.com/website-owners**

Blog posts

At www.debbie-emmitt.com, I regularly publish blog posts that focus on a particular aspect of creating or maintaining your online platform.

If you subscribe to my mailing list, you'll get a heads-up when the latest blog post is available, plus occasional extra news and titbits that will help you to be a website guru!

To sign up, visit **www.debbie-emmitt.com/signup**

2 – Your Site Goal

Have one main goal for your site at any one time and make this especially clear on your homepage.

Objectives

You may have several objectives in mind for your website, such as:

- promoting your editing and proofreading services
- connecting with potential clients (e.g. authors, businesses, publishers)
- helping other editors
- growing your email subscriber list
- increasing your visitor count

While it's fine to try to achieve more than one of the above, the best approach is to choose one main goal and make that the focus of your site, particularly on your homepage.

Main goal focus

If your main goal is to promote your editing services and a secondary goal is to increase your subscriber list, you will dedicate a large proportion of homepage space to marketing your services (e.g. your best testimonial, an image of you at work, short text about your services and a link to your services page).

Your secondary goal can be met too, but don't let it compete for space with your services marketing content. Instead of taking up prime real estate with your sign-up form on the homepage, have a clearly visible button in the header or footer so that it isn't jostling for pole position.

Figure 1 – Jessica Brown's homepage has a primary goal of encouraging potential clients to contact her to discuss their book. The heading is written from the client's point of view, and the text clearly explains Jessica's target audience and services. The call to action ('Make Me an Author') goes to the Contact page.

Shifting focus

At certain times in your marketing calendar, you may want to shift the focus of your site from one goal to another (e.g. if you're speaking at a conference or about to launch a passive income product (PIP)). Just be clear about what your main goal is at any one time, or visitors will feel as if they're being attacked by a scatter gun.

If you're not sure what to focus on, think about:

- where you are currently in your marketing calendar

- the size of your email subscription list, if you have one

- what you'd most like people to do when they're on your site

- your audience and their needs (we'll look at this in the next section).

3 – Audience

You have a matter of seconds to attract the attention of your visitors before they leave.

While it continues to be a contentious issue as to whether our attention span is dwindling or not, it cannot be disputed that there are more 'on-hand' temptations to distract us than ever before.[4] People are expecting results from websites in an increasingly shorter window of time, whether waiting for a page to load or finding what they came for.

The key to ensuring they stay is making your website work for them, not for you. To do this, you need to understand who they are and what they want from your site.

What's in it for me?

You're thinking about your audience for a reason, of course.

---

[4] 'Are attention spans really collapsing? Data shows UK public are worried – but also see benefits from technology', King's College London. 2022 [Online]. Available: https://www.kcl.ac.uk/news/are-attention-spans-really-collapsing-data-shows-uk-public-are-worried-but-also-see-benefits-from-technology [Accessed: 11 March 2023]

If you give them what they want, your conversion rates are more likely to increase. 'Conversion' refers to how many people sign up to your mailing list, hit Submit on your enquiry form, or fulfil another action you would like them to complete.

There are formulae you can use to calculate your conversion rate. The most basic one is number of conversions divided by number of sessions. For example:

1,000 clicks divided by 10,000 sessions = 0.10 (10%)

If you'd like to calculate more complicated versions of this, use your favourite search engine to find what you need.

User personas

Creating user personas for your website will help you with every future decision, including writing content, selecting images, deciding on navigation headings and creating calls to action.

A user persona is a fancy term for a fictional character typical of one segment of your audience. Before you begin to write your personas, you need to work out who your target audiences are. These will be largely determined by the kind of editing you offer, especially if you have a niche.

It would be impossible to list all the possible target audiences for an editor website, but some common ones are:

- self-published authors

- publishers

- academics

- entrepreneurs/businesses

- fellow editors looking for inspiration and advice.

For each target audience, there may be more than one persona. For example, the 'self-published authors' audience may sub-divide into multiple personas depending on style of English (UK, US, Australian, Canadian, etc.), level of writing/publishing experience, genre, location and more.

You could go overboard with this process and sub-divide ad infinitum. The trick is to pinpoint the main segments of your audience, then develop personas to act as stereotypes for those segments. A healthy number to begin with is three to five, then you may wish to be more granular later.

People and markets are not static, so review your personas regularly, especially if you are introducing a new service or have decided to focus on a niche.

Basic personas

The simplest personas are a paragraph of text describing the key points about that audience segment. These can be fun to write!

Three basic personas for a fiction editor's website could be:

- John Smith is a 65-year-old retired teacher who has written his first novel. He is a self-taught writer, learning the craft from websites and online courses, and doesn't know how the editing process works.

- Jenny Jones is a 30-year-old successful self-published author looking for an editor for her tenth book. Her previous editor has left the profession for personal reasons, and Jenny is keen to find a trustworthy editor to do a first-rate job on her latest book, and potentially subsequent ones.

- Alice Evans runs an independent publishing house and is looking for an editor to join her small team. She saw your name in a book that you edited previously, searched for you online and arrived at your website. She's keen to find out if you're a good fit for her business.

For each persona, it is helpful to give them a fictional name and photo (search online for 'copyright-free persona images'), so you can picture them when you're working on your site.

Detailed personas

Once you've got the hang of thinking in terms of personas, it's useful to flesh them out. Think about:

- what they're looking for on your site
- what type of content they produce
- how long they have been writing/how established the company is
- relevant likes and dislikes.

Beware of going into too much detail. They need to remain archetypes for the audience segment they represent. Knowing that John Smith likes Wensleydale cheese probably isn't helpful when it comes to his behaviour on your site (unless you only edit books about cheese—that would be a specific niche!).

User journeys

Once you have your user personas (basic or detailed), think about the journeys they would take to arrive at the ideal outcome.

These outcomes could include:

- contacting you to book an editing service
- signing up to your newsletter
- filling out your contact form.

Visitors will not always enter your site from the homepage. Depending on where they have come from (search engine, another site, manually entered your web address), they could begin at any page on your site. This is important because if you've planned a user journey only from the homepage, you could miss out a crucial call to action on a subpage, losing that potential client or newsletter sign-up.

Ideally, you will create at least one journey for each persona, and you're likely to find that each will have more than one. For example, John Smith does not yet subscribe to your newsletter, so two of his user journeys could be to sign up and to fill out your contact form.

A user journey for John's sign-up to your newsletter could look like this:

Figure 2 – Example of a user journey

Just as with user personas, there is not one typical template to use. Some people prefer a tabular layout, where each column is a stage in the journey. Others use a flowchart approach as in Figure 2, or a simple bulleted list. As long as you've logged the key stages, don't lose sleep over the layout.

User journeys will help you to streamline your site. For example, mapping John's journey to subscribe to your newsletter may highlight the lack of a sign-up button on your homepage. If John must navigate to your Contact page before he finds what he's looking for, you may have missed out on a new subscriber.

Personas are also invaluable when you make any change to your business. If you're considering introducing a manuscript evaluation service, for example, consider what each of your personas would think about it. This need only take a few minutes and can help you to 'get outside your head' and spot issues that would otherwise have remained invisible to you.

Usability testing

Once you know your key audience segments and the journeys they will take, it's a good idea to subject your site to some usability testing. This will quickly pinpoint problem areas.

There are three ways in which you can carry out usability testing:

- **Moderated in-person** – the tester sits with the participant.
- **Moderated remote** – the tester is in a different location to the participant and the test is viewed 'live' using screen-sharing or computer-monitoring software.
- **Unmoderated remote** – a series of tests are set, and participants take them at a time convenient to them. Videos of the testing are viewed later by the tester.

Owners of large complex sites often spend vast sums on different types of usability tests to discover issues encountered by visitors. Unless your editor site is extensive, or you suspect major usability problems, you just need to do some simple testing.

"Socrates said, 'Know thyself.' I say, 'Know thy users.' And guess what? They don't think like you do."

— *Joshua Brewer, digital designer*

Setting tasks

This is where the user journeys you've established will come in handy. Prepare some tasks for test participants, based on the journeys, then find some willing testers.

Participants

Ideally, the participants will be from your target audiences, but if your site is fairly small, it may not be worth the time and expense to locate them. As long as the participants are not very familiar with your site, their test results will be useful.

An example of a simple task would be:

1. Go to www.myeditorsite.com.

2. Find out whether I offer sample edits.

Facilitator

This is the person who oversees moderated tests. Facilitating is ideally carried out by an impartial person.

You are too emotionally invested in your site to carry out the testing, especially if you designed and built it yourself. This may lead you to subconsciously help the participants with their tasks.

Also, if they know of your connection with the site, they may not feel free to be completely honest, and you will have wasted time and resources in testing.

Important points to remember about usability tests:

- It is the site, not the participant, that is being tested.

- The facilitator must not speak during the tasks, or they may inadvertently influence the results.

- The participant should be encouraged to continuously think out loud.

A/B testing

This is comparative testing, where you offer two versions of the element to be tested, for example, different page layouts.

It can be run as a task-setting exercise, where participants are asked to work through a task, or set of tasks, first on one design and then on another. Alternatively, two different sets of people see one of the two designs.

Pros and cons of different A/B testing approaches

Participant method	Pros	Cons
Same people see both designs	Fewer participants are needed. If you'd like five results for each design, you only need five people.	Users aren't coming fresh to the second design (mitigate this by alternating from person to person which design is seen first).
Different people – one group sees Design A, a separate group sees Design B. Both groups complete identical tasks.	All participants see both designs for the first time.	You need double the number of participants for the same number of results as the other approach.

Testing subscriber email content

A/B testing is not restricted to usability tests on your website. It can be used in many areas of your online presence. For example, your email subscription service (e.g. MailChimp, ConvertKit) may offer A/B testing as part of your package. This is a good way to test if subscribers are more likely to act on an element in your emails if it were a different colour or font, in a different position, or worded differently.

It's highly advisable to test one element at a time, otherwise you won't know which one has influenced the results. For example, if you were to change the position of a button and its colour, and one version had a far higher click-through rate (number of people clicking from your email to where the link takes them), you wouldn't know if the colour or position had the greater influence.

If you have a long list of subscribers, you can A/B test a small number per mailing, then send the more successful version to the rest. Over time, you can build up a picture of colours, positions and fonts that most encourage people to click through to your site or wherever your call to action takes them.

You can A/B test just about every element of your newsletter: subject line (to test for open rate), email copy, calls to action and more.

Testing tools

If you get the user-testing bug, there are many different angles from which you can analyse user data. The more you get to know what your users are doing when they visit your site, the more you can speed up their user journey and give them what they want (and guide them to where you'd like them to be).

Some of these other methods include:

- **heat maps and click maps** – tracking where your visitors are scrolling and clicking

- **eye tracking** – seeing what page elements are most engaging

- **analytics software** – e.g. Google Analytics.

If you enter a search term like 'web usability testing tools' into your favourite search engine, you'll find the latest ones available that can help you with all the above. Some are open source and free, others are a paid service usually with a free trial at the start.

4 – Site Structure

Structure your site according to the needs of your audience, not your own.

Put yourself in the shoes of one of your key audiences, let's say a self-published author looking for an editor. They will come to your site with a specific intention. This may be:

- to find out what services you offer
- to discover the cost of your copyediting service
- to contact you.

If you make it easy for them to complete their intended task, it will create a positive, lasting impression on them. They will be more likely to spend time on your site, interact with you (e.g. signing up for updates) and return.

Streamline your site

If you have a small site, it will be easy to keep it neat and logical. Larger sites may need a bit of housekeeping.

If you're a fairly new editor, or if you don't offer online information or resources over and above your services, you may simply have the following pages (exact titles can be tweaked to suit your style):

- Home
- About
- Services
- Contact

You may also decide to have a blog on your site (if you're sure you can dedicate the time to keep it updated regularly), and information about any events you're hosting or presenting at (webinars, conferences, etc.). You may have subpages below these top-level pages, for example, a page for each of your services.

If you're more established, you may have a section dedicated to courses you offer, books and resources either for sale or as free downloads, information about your podcast, and/or a portfolio page.

You'll find more details about what you can include on each page in the Content section of this guide.

Remove clutter

If your site has been around a while, it may have grown larger than it needs to be. Take a moment to consider if you need all your content. Do your visitors really want to know about your favourite wine or where you last went on holiday? Obviously, if these facts directly relate to the kind of content you edit (food and drink, or travel), feel free to include them!

An ideal way to decide what to cull is to look at your site analytics (e.g. Google Analytics). Hold a magnifying glass to those pages that receive little or no traffic. If people are leaving as soon as they arrive, try to work out why. If these are one of the core pages mentioned above, you need to improve them (by following the advice in this guide) to keep those visit numbers up. If they are not core pages, you need to decide if it's time to kill the little darlings.

Be a friend to search engines

Ensuring your site has a clean, logical structure is about more than making just your human visitors happy. It will also make search engines ecstatic. Your site will rank higher in search engine results if it is easy for the search bots to crawl your site, easily finding all your juicy content.

User-friendly navigation

Your primary navigation is called the 'navigation bar', or 'navbar' if you want to get friendly. Most sites display this horizontally at the top of each page, so users expect it to be there. That's not to say it cannot be elsewhere, but if you want to buck the trend, make sure you carry out usability testing to check your visitors can quickly find what they need.

If you have a large site, you may also have submenus.

Look at your navigation options. Would someone coming to your site for the first time know what they will get when they select something? Are your titles hard to read because they're longer than necessary?

If you work through the following improvements, you'll soon have menus that sing to your visitors:

- **Shorten titles** – Keep text short but meaningful. This will help visitors quickly scan the options. Rather than 'Read my biography', how about simply 'Biography' or 'About'?

- **Reduce options** – Too many options can confuse visitors, and long menus can cause usability issues on mobile devices with smaller screens.

- **Avoid jargon** – Don't use terms that only make sense to you or people in the editing industry. This includes acronyms.

- **Order according to users' needs** – Don't list your navbar or submenu items alphabetically, or in order of importance to you. By putting items of most interest or import to your visitors first, you will help them quickly find what they need.

Editor and author

Many editors are also authors. If this is you, each 'hat' will need an online presence, which may affect your site structure. How you present your two roles will depend on whether you wish to keep them completely distinct, or whether you'd prefer a link of some kind.

There are three approaches to consider:

Separate websites, no linking

You may prefer to keep your roles of editor and author totally separate (maybe you write kids' books but edit academic content, so there is no benefit in cross-marketing). In this case, both roles will need a website, each with distinct branding, structure and content. Apply the advice in this guide to each site in turn. For advice specific to your author site, check out this book's sister guide, *Improve Your Author Website*.

Separate websites, cross-linking

You may prefer to cross-promote your roles of editor and writer, especially if you write the same kind of content or in the same genre as you edit. In this case, you may choose to have a separate site for each role to create individual branding and write copy targeted at the respective audiences, then link between the two sites for cross-promotion purposes.

Same website, different sections

If your two roles share the same audience, at least in part, and/or you don't have the time or resources to manage two websites, you may choose to keep all your content on one site. You could have an over-arching homepage with links to subpages or subdomains for each role or have items in the navigation that point readers to your writing and editing sections.

I am an editor/proofreader and a mystery author. Currently, I have one website for both roles, with one About page, one Contact page, and separate sections for my editing services and writing. Ideally, I would prefer a separate site for my author activities, as there isn't much of a crossover between the audiences. However, due to the extra time it would take to manage two sites (plus two newsletters and two blogs), I have stuck with one site for now. If my writing takes off, I will probably separate my two roles online and cross-link.

Figure 3 – Tèmítáyò Olófinlúà is a writer, editor and academic. Her website does a great job of clearly pointing people to each of these distinct roles. There is a drop-down list under 'Work' in the main navigation, plus a separate 'Services' option for people to discover her editing services in more detail.

Figure 4 – Rachel Rowlands is an editor and author. She makes this clear in her header, as part of her logo, and she has 'My Books' and 'Editorial Services' clearly marked in the main navigation.

5 – Site-Wide Principles

There are some general principles of best practice to apply across your whole site, encompassing design, content and accessibility.

Consistency

A consistent website will look professional and have a strong sense of identity. Potential clients will have confidence in your ability to deliver quality work; fellow editors will have confidence in your advice (e.g. your blog posts) because your site is professional. Treat your website like sample content. If there are errors or unnecessarily wordy sentences, potential clients will be put off.

External consistency

Ensuring your site is consistent with web best practices and shares common traits with other sites will show you as credible and will save your visitors time and frustration. It will also help you to remain compliant with accessibility guidelines.

There are many best practices for websites, covering aspects including design, colours, text and calls to action. These are not there to make your life difficult (even though it may seem like it!) or your site boring and unimaginative.

Just as story structure offers a framework within which writers can bend the rules, so is the case with best practice on the web. Once you know the rules and understand why they exist, you can confidently innovate.

If you adhere to web best practices, your visitors will feel welcome, happier and adept at finding what they need. They will spend less time working out how to use your site and more time engaging with your content.

If you work through this guide and apply everything within it to your site, you will achieve a high level of external consistency.

Internal consistency

Keeping your site consistent within itself will give your online presence a strong sense of identity and will instil trust in your visitors.

If the look and feel is different from page to page, they'll wonder if they're still on your site and will get confused.

Your site will also look unprofessional and potential clients will wonder how much attention you would pay to their manuscript or copy.

Internal consistency refers to factors particular to your site, including:

- colours

- fonts

- spacing between elements

- position of menus

- headings

- image sizes (all thumbnails the same size, for example)

- form components (buttons, links, text input fields)

- icons (same family)

If you have a strong brand on any printed materials, such as business cards, carry this across to your site so that readers coming from the printed version of you to the online one will have a consistent experience. Alternatively, update your business cards to match your posh new website!

Methods to achieve internal consistency include:

- using templates (this is made easy with platforms like WordPress)

- regularly checking your site

- when creating a new page that is similar to an existing one (e.g. a new service page), refer to the original one to ensure you aren't going off piste.

Up-to-date content

This depends on how much time you can dedicate to your site. Before you decide you have very little time for this, bear in mind that your site is the first port of call for many of your potential clients. Plan regular chunks of time to dedicate to this crucial marketing tool.

A blog is a good way to ensure you have fresh content, but if you don't update it regularly, it can do your site more harm than good. Visitors may assume your whole site is out of date if your last blog entry is dated six months ago.

Plan

It is worth putting a web marketing plan in place. This can be a simple calendar on which you mark when you will update your site with new content, images, news and blog posts. Some editors may wish to update on at least a weekly basis, others may prefer monthly. In any case, scheduling the work will make you more likely to achieve it and will reduce any pressure you may be feeling about your site slipping in this regard.

Also include in your plan when to remove content that expires on a certain date, for example, an event listing.

6 – Site Design

The look and feel of your site should not distract from the content.

First impressions

Research from 2011 (and I'm sure it hasn't changed!) has shown that first impressions of a website are made in just 50 milliseconds.[5] Of those first impressions, 94% are design related.[6] This shows it is the design that reels in your visitors (and good content that makes them stay).

Think about what you want those first impressions to be. When a visitor snatches that first glimpse of your site, what do you want them to feel?

---

[5] Gitte Lindgaard, Gary Fernandes, Cathy Dudek & J. Brown, 'Attention web designers: You have 50 milliseconds to make a good first impression!'. 2011 [Online]. *Behaviour & Information Technology*, 25:2, 115-126, DOI: https://doi.org/10.1080/01449290500330448 [Accessed: 11 March 2023]

[6] Findings of 2004 study carried out by Northumbria and Sheffield Universities, UK, analysed in online article by Peep Laja, First impressions matter: the importance of great visual design, *CXL*. 2022 (updated) [Online]. Available: https://conversionxl.com/blog/first-impressions-matter-the-importance-of-great-visual-design/ [Accessed: 11 March 2023]

Maybe:

- trust (in you as an editor, as a person, or in the site if online payment or collection of personal data is involved)
- impressed (by the site and your previous clients' testimonials)
- reassured
- curiosity about how you can help them
- all the above

Once you know what initial impression you'd like to make (remember, we're talking about that very first impression in those first 50 milliseconds), think about the colours and layout that may give rise to that.

You can then mock up some test pages (homepage or other) and run a usability-testing session to see which is most successful, or which users like best.

They may not even know why they have a certain preference; it can be enough for you to know that it's the most subconsciously appealing design to your target audience.

This type of usability testing could be done remotely using your mailing list if you have one.

Similar ... but different

While there is a place for crazy innovation and radical colour schemes, this is a risky strategy when applied to most websites. In the early days of the web, all manner of backgrounds, fonts and layouts were available, but the web playground has since settled down to a more mature approach (in most professional arenas, at least).

> "The more familiar we are with something, the more we like it."
>
> — *Robert Zajonc, social psychologist*

If you want your visitors to feel at home on your site and quickly find what they need, it's not a good idea to swim too hard against the tide when it comes to certain website principles.

This doesn't mean your site is doomed to look like every other editor's site, but it does mean there are certain conventions your users will expect you to follow. Some of these have already been described in previous sections, others are covered through the rest of the guide.

Figure 5 – The Book Butchers' site design is anything but conventional. However, they stick to certain best practices such as their logo top left that links to the homepage, and the main site navigation across the top of each page (where users will expect to find it).

Use white space

White space doesn't literally mean the colour of the space on your page must be white. Also known as negative space, it refers to parts of your page where there is no text, just the background colour or background image.

Before the widespread use of mobiles and tablets, it was best practice to keep webpages short and put crucial information above the fold (the point at which a user starts scrolling). This often led to cramped, busy designs, with a lot going on in a small space.

Since the explosion of tablet and mobile web browsing, and the wider variety of screen sizes that came with this, people are far more used to vertical scrolling (although horizontal scrolling is still a massive no-no).

This trend towards scrolling gives you freedom to use white space, allowing your content to breathe. If your visitors are faced with a page crammed with content vying for their attention, they will be overwhelmed, not know what to choose and probably leave.

Keep it simple

As already mentioned, it takes your visitors just 50 milliseconds to form an impression of your site. Therefore, it stands to reason that the simpler the design, the more easily visitors will engage with it.

A quick online search for 'award-winning websites' will further highlight the fact that simplicity wins.

To keep your design simple, try the following tips.

Use white/negative space

As already mentioned, this will keep your site looking 'clean' and give users the space to find what they're looking for, or to be drawn to what you'd like to highlight.

> "A designer knows he has achieved perfection not when there is nothing left to add, but when there is nothing left to take away."
>
> — *Antoine de Saint-Exupéry, author, illustrator and aviator*

Remove redundant elements

You can pinpoint these in several ways, including the following:

- Try to look at your site through your visitors' eyes (use the personas you've created to help you). Which buttons, images, boxes or links are of little use or interest to them?

- If anything appears twice on the same page, remove one instance of it. There are some exceptions to this, such as a sign-up link in your top navbar and in your footer.

- Use a heat-mapping tool or click tracker to see where your users' attention is drawn the least. Decide if this is because the item is in the wrong place or if it can simply be removed.

Don't include unnecessary, fancy elements just because you can

A spinning image of a book you recently edited may seem a good idea at the time, but users will not thank you for it. These types of gimmicks can be distracting and annoying, and they add a layer of complexity to your site that has a higher chance of breaking.

Make it responsive

Responsive design is about making sure your site functions well and looks good across as many browsers, platforms and devices as possible.

See 'Responsive design' in the 'Site Performance' chapter (Chapter 12) for more details.

7 – Content

Content is king. Your visitors will thank you (via longer visits, email subscriptions and enquiries) for getting it right.

Your site design draws in visitors, but your content holds them there, encourages them to explore more of your site and keeps them coming back.

> "Content precedes design. Design in the absence of content is not design, it's decoration."
>
> *- Jeffrey Zeldman, web designer*

There are certain pages that visitors to an editor's site expect to see, but you can add custom ones too, depending on your niche, personality and target audience.

Home

Although your homepage is not necessarily the starting point for your visitors (they may have arrived at your About page via a Google search, for example), it is likely to be the most visited page on your site. It is the URL (web address) that you promote and where visitors go if they get lost on your site (but you can drastically reduce the likelihood of disoriented visitors if you have a neat, logical structure! See 'Site Structure' (Chapter 4)).

Think of your homepage like a magazine cover. It's not a place where users hang out for long; it showcases the items of most interest and encourages visitors to dig deeper. It is, therefore, of vital importance to make it easy to use.

Keep it simple

Don't feel you have to cram everything in, or visitors will become blind to it all. Consider which parts of your site are of most interest to your audience and make sure these have a homepage spot. Remember the user journeys of your audiences and put the first steps on your homepage.

Your homepage is valuable real estate. Each piece of content must be working for you. If it isn't, get rid of it.

Allow scrolling

As I mentioned in 'Site Design' (Chapter 6), when I talked about the importance of white space, today's users expect to scroll.

Give yourself room to include essential content without feeling everything must be at the top of the page (just make sure the call to action for your site's goal is visible when the page first loads).

Say who you are

More than just your name should be at the top of the page. Give visitors a clear, concise idea of your niche. For example: "Joanna Bloggs, editor of financial content".

Figure 6 – Sarah Calfee's homepage and header for her editing company, Three Little Words, leaves visitors in no doubt as to the fact she edits romance fiction.

Promote your services

Many visitors will come to your site to find information about your editing services, and, for most editors, promoting their offerings will be the primary site goal. Put this information front and centre; don't make people go searching for it.

Outline what you offer and link to your top-level services page. You could also include the testimonial you're most proud of.

Include a call to action

A call to action is content that induces visitors to act, e.g. a 'Sign up' button.

As the most visited page on your site, the homepage is a crucial conversion area, so use it wisely. If you have an email newsletter, make sure people can sign up from your homepage.

No welcome message

Show, don't tell. People don't need to be told they're on your site; they already know. Similarly, avoid telling them what they will find on your site. Show them. Don't write copy like: "Welcome to the homepage of Joanna Bloggs. Here you will find…"

Make it clear who you are and what you do in your header, or high up in the page body (see 'Say who you are' on the previous page), and point the way to key content through featured links and calls to action.

About

This is where you get to tell your visitors about yourself in a unique, captivating way. Your social media bio may need revising for your website to ensure you're hitting the right tone with your site visitors. Include the kind of content you edit, why you're qualified to do so, and your skills and experience.

If previous clients have done well with Amazon ratings and reviews or won writing prizes, let people know.

List any professional organisations you're a member of, e.g. the Chartered Institute of Editing and Proofreading (CIEP), and state your level of membership, if applicable.

Look at other editors' bio pages for inspiration, but make sure your own personality shines through. Potential clients want to know what it's like to work with *you*, as opposed to other editors. If you come across as friendly, supportive and experienced, this will go a long way to them taking the next step of contacting you.

Some editors prefer to write their About page in first person as it feels more personal; others prefer third person as it sounds more authoritative. It's up to you which approach you choose.

Include a photo of yourself so people feel more engaged with you. Aim for a friendly, professional look. Think about your brand, site colours and target audience. Smile, consider what is in the background, and don't use a holiday snap. Ideally, arrange a professional photoshoot so you can give a credible impression and have several poses, locations and activities to use across your site.

Use the same profile photo of yourself across all your media outlets (Facebook, LinkedIn, online directories, etc.) to ensure consistency of brand.

Hey there! I'm Kris.

Copyeditor extraordinaire and writer on all things from web words to wanderlust, creativity to compassion, location independence to language love.

IT'S GREAT YOU'RE HERE!

If you love words anywhere near as much as I do, you're in the right place.

Whether it's writing for yourself, writing for others, or just an appreciation of beautiful language, we're gonna hit it off just fine!

After playing word nerd through my twenties and nabbing a couple of linguistics quals, I bounced off to London enthusiastically. Only to have the stuffing kicked out of me by a pretty draining day job.

I started out as a staff writer there, but soon knew the **entrepreneurial life** was more my cup of tea. (*Actually, I prefer a flat white, how un-English of me! But back to the story...*)

Figure 7 – Kris Emery's About page has a professional, smiling image in keeping with her brand. The page copy is relaxed and informal, reflecting Kris's bubbly personality and individual voice.

Services

If you offer different levels of editing (e.g. developmental, copyediting, proofreading), an ideal approach to this section is to have a top-level page that outlines each service, with links to subpages that go into more detail.

On each service page, include testimonials from previous clients, a description of the service and a link to your contact page. You could also add an image, maybe of you working hard on a client's copy.

Whether or not you include pricing information is entirely up to you. Some editors prefer to ask potential clients to contact them for a bespoke quote; other editors display prices on their site. I provide 'indicative prices' to give potential clients a rough idea of how much their project may cost, while making it clear the actual cost may go up or down, depending on how much work is involved.

You could also include information about books or projects you have worked on in your Services section, or you could provide a portfolio as a separate top-level section.

Figure 8 – Candida Bradford's Services page clearly lists each service she offers, with a short description and price per 1,000 words. For each service, she provides a 'Learn More' button that links to a subpage containing more information.

Contact

It's crucial to provide a way for potential clients, fellow editors and other audiences to get in touch with you. If you aren't easy to get hold of, you could be missing out on your next favourite project or networking opportunities.

Include a Contact link in your main navigation that takes visitors to a page with your preferred ways for them to get in touch. This may be a contact form, email address and/or social media links.

It's a good idea to give people more than one way to get in touch. This provides a backup in case one method fails and gives your visitors a chance to pick their preferred method.

If you are active on social media, include links from your Contact page to all parts of your platform (LinkedIn, Facebook, Instagram, etc.). If you're just starting out, there's no need to be active on every one of these; you'll dilute your presence and will overwhelm yourself. Pick the one that works best for you and build up slowly.

Contact form or email address?

Some editors offer a contact form and an email address, allowing visitors to choose their preferred method. Most, however, stick to one or the other.

If using a contact form, keep it as short as possible (to avoid people being put off by a lengthy form and to comply with data protection laws – we must only collect the personal data we need for the purpose at hand).

There are pros and cons to each method.

Contact form

Pros

- Your email address isn't published for spambots to take advantage of.

- You can embed the form on a page then link to it from anywhere on your site.

- If kept short (just email address and space for message, possibly also a name field), most people will be happy to fill it in.

- It looks more professional than just an email address.

- You can protect yourself against spambots to a certain degree by adding a CAPTCHA field (users have to prove they're human by ticking a box or entering text), or by adding a hidden field (a honeypot) that spambots will detect but humans won't. Make sure the honeypot field is clearly marked for people using screen readers.

- Visitors don't have to open their email software; they can stay on your site. This is a bonus for you and them!

- You can set the text for the subject line of all messages, so you can see at a glance in your inbox which emails are from your website.

- Depending on how you build your form or which plugins you use, you can add extra features such as a newsletter sign-up box (familiarise yourself with data protection laws, e.g. don't have the box checked by default).

- You may have a PA who also needs to see emails sent to you. With a form, you can make sure they also receive the form responses.

- Visitors receive an acknowledgement that their query has been sent.

Cons

- Some visitors are put off by having to complete a form, especially if it is long.

- Forms can be seen as less personal.

Email address

Pros

- Visitors can easily see your email address and add you to their contacts.

- Some people may prefer to contact you using their email client.

- Users have a record of the email sent.

Cons

- Spambots may harvest your email address if it isn't encoded. To counter this, some editors display their address in full and don't link it, e.g. "joe at joebloggs dot com". While this will fool spambots, it isn't as convenient for users, who have to cut and paste then adjust the email address, or manually type it in, which could lead to typos.

- Any attachments, email signatures or other files associated with emails sent to you will take up space in your inbox.

- Anyone can send an infected file to your inbox.

- The links open the users' default mail application, which may not be their preferred option.

- There is usually no autoreply to acknowledge acceptance of the email, although this can be set up.

Figure 9 – Denise Cowle's 'Contact' page is a great example of a short form that is easy to complete. The email address provided is not a live link, so spambots can't follow it. She also provides a physical mailing address and linked icons to her social media pages.

Blog

Why have a blog?

A review by HubSpot found that business websites with a blog attract 55% more traffic than those without one, 97% more inbound links and, wait for it, 434% more indexed pages (by search engines).[7]

It seems reasonable to assume this 'rule' would extend to editor sites too. Why?

- A blog creates regular, fresh content which helps the search engine optimisation (SEO) of your site. It's a signal to search bots that your site is up to date, and it increases the keywords that are relevant to your site. Hence, you'll come up more frequently in searches. In addition, the more useful and/or interesting content you have, the longer people will stay on your site – another factor that search bots love and the search engine algorithms take notice of.

- A blog allows you to add extra content to your site without cluttering up your homepage or bloating your navigation. This keeps your site visually appealing and organised, encouraging return visits.

- Each week, fortnight or month – however often you blog (I'd recommend releasing a post at least once a month to keep top of your audience's mind) – you can link to your new post from social media, driving traffic to your site.

---

[7] Rick Burnes, 'Study shows business blogging leads to 55% more website visitors', *Hubspot*. Originally published 2009, updated 2022 [Online]. Available: https://blog.hubspot.com/blog/tabid/6307/bid/5014/study-shows-business-blogging-leads-to-55-more-website-visitors.aspx [Accessed: 11 March 2023]

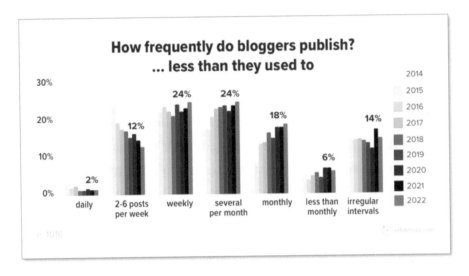

Figure 10 – Orbit Media Studios' research shows that most bloggers post weekly or a few times a month.

Blog post ideas

If you're stuck for ideas on what to write, read on for some pointers.

Answer your audience's questions

The primary audiences for most editors' sites are potential clients (depending on your style of editing, these could be self-published authors, publishers, businesses, entrepreneurs and more) and fellow editors.

There are plenty of sources you can use to discover what your typical visitor wants to know:

- pre-existing queries in your inbox

- comments on previous blog posts or on your social media profiles

- sites like Quora and Reddit – good sources of pain points for different niches

- comments on other editors' blogs – especially those who work on similar content to you

- LinkedIn, Facebook, X (the platform formerly known as Twitter) and other social media platforms – these are rich hunting grounds for what people want to know from you and other editors. Check out groups like Ask A Book Editor on Facebook.

Show your knowledge of elements of writing

This leads on from the previous section about answering your audience's questions. Writing blog posts on aspects of grammar, spelling, punctuation, and indeed any area of writing that people struggle with, can do wonders for your SEO, as people in your target audience will be searching for answers to questions about language and writing.

Try to find a niche topic, something that not every editor is writing about, then make your blog post the definitive article on that issue. This will push your post to the top of online search results for that topic and drive lots of traffic to your site. For example, my blog post on number ranges attracts almost one-third of my entire site traffic and is at the top of Google's search results for 'number ranges'.

Some of the visitors to your blog posts will be potential clients who may discover you're the editor for them.

Write book reviews

If you edit fiction or non-fiction books, remember that authors (your target clients) are also avid readers. They will be interested in reading your book reviews and will be impressed by your knowledge of story structure, plot, character arcs and the craft of writing in general.

At the end of each review, encourage visitors to sign up to your mailing list so they don't miss your next recommendation. Be sure to contact the author whose book you are reviewing. While (as far as I'm aware) this is not a legal obligation, it's good practice and polite to do so. You should also check they're happy for you to use any images you've selected (book cover, author headshot, etc.). What's more, you can mention that you'd be grateful if they would share a link to your review on their social media channels, which will generate traffic to your site!

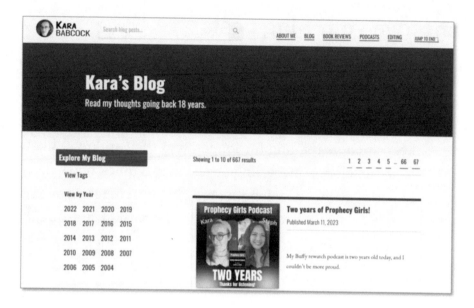

Figure 11 – Kara Babcock has been blogging for an impressive 18 years (and counting). She writes about her life, politics, books, gender issues, freelancing and more.

Share personal stories

This may not be for everyone – it depends how much of your life you'd like to share with your readers. Avoid posting personal details online, e.g. names of pets and family, dates of birth, as these could potentially be used against you by hackers and other nefarious people. **If you don't need to share personal information, then don't.**

Many visitors will enjoy seeing these insights into your life. Only share as much as you're comfortable sharing. Rule of thumb: What would you be happy telling the town gossip?

Improve your blog posts

Follow these tips to improve your blog posts, and see an increase in pageviews, visit duration and audience engagement:

- **Aim for long-form posts rather than brief updates** – This keeps people reading for longer, and they are more likely to share a long, interesting article than a quick news flash. Experts say the ideal length for a blog post in terms of SEO is 1,760–2,400 words, but equally important are quality substance, keywords in the headings, and other factors.[8]

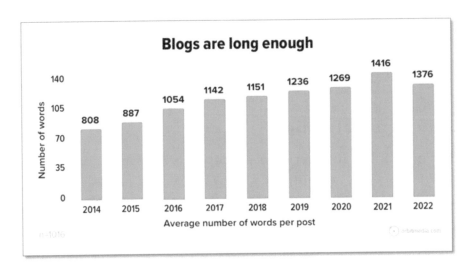

Figure 12 – Orbit Media Studios' research shows the average length of blog posts has generally increased over time.

---

[8] 'How long should a blog post be for SEO in 2023?', Hook Agency. 2023 [Online]. Available: https://hookagency.com/blog/blog-length/ [Accessed: 11 March 2023]

- **Post regularly** – There is no hard and fast rule as to frequency of posting, but I'd recommend at least once a month. If you can't devote this time, it's best not to have a blog as it will look out of date and will do little to help your SEO.

- **Keep sentences and paragraphs short, and use subheadings** – This will keep readers engaged and enable them to scan-read the post.

- **Include images, videos, audio, graphs, etc.** – (not necessarily all in the same post!). At the very least, have one large image at the top. While images aren't essential for a post to rank well in search results, they certainly help.[9]

- **Breathe new life into old posts** – If you have a large archive of posts, update the most popular ones to keep your audience and search engines happy (neither party is keen on old content!).

- **Send your email subscribers an update with a link to each new post** – This will drive traffic to your site and make them feel appreciated, as they will always be aware when a new post is ready. If you don't have a mailing list, seriously consider setting one up.

---

[9] James Parsons, 'Are blog post images necessary for articles to rank well?', *Content Powered*. 2021 [Online]. Available: https://www.contentpowered.com/blog/blog-images-necessary-rank/ [Accessed: 11 March 2023]

- **Feature your latest blog posts on your homepage** – This keeps the page fresh, encourages return visits and is great for SEO (because the homepage doesn't get stagnant). Ideally, this should update automatically to save you the admin hassle each time you post.

Other pages

I've described the most advisable minimum pages to include on your site, but you don't have to stop there.

The main rule of thumb is to avoid filling your site with vanity content only of interest to you. It will clutter your site, detract attention from your audience's key user journeys and may lose you a sign-up, client booking or sale.

If there is other content you'd like to include on your site, go for it, while always bearing in mind your site goal and main audiences.

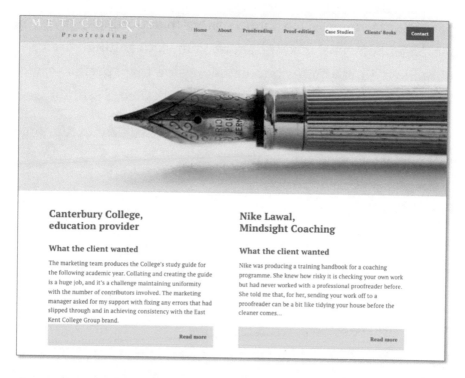

Figure 13 – Yasmin Yarwood of Meticulous Proofreading provides case studies on her website, so potential clients can have a detailed look at some of her past projects and get a flavour of what it's like to work with her.

Other elements

Testimonials

Do you take notice of reviews when buying anything online? Is that a resounding 'Yes'? So do your visitors. Testimonials are an example of social proof. If someone else has enjoyed something, we're more likely to buy.

Place your testimonials in context rather than putting them all on one page. Someone reading about your copyediting service is more likely to read a testimonial alongside that specific service than if they have to click on a menu option called 'Testimonials'.

It's also a good idea to put one or two particularly exceptional testimonials on your homepage.

Header

Your header is a key part of your site. It's the first thing visitors see when your page loads – when that crucial initial impression is made.

The term 'header' used to refer to the area from the top of the page down to, and including, the navbar (main menu). While this is still often the case, increasingly the area is expanding to incorporate more of the page body, as images become larger and designs become more encompassing.

Whatever you choose to do with your site header, here are some tips to help you strike the right tone and layout:

- **Make your business name immediately obvious** – If it isn't in the middle of the header, put it to the left. Don't place it to the right; this is not where visitors expect to see branding information.

- **Use relevant imagery** – If you use a header image, ensure this reflects the type of content you edit. If you edit across many genres or topics, use more abstract imagery, or an image related to editing but not a particular topic.

- **Place input boxes top right** – If your site has an internal search or a login function, users will expect to find this top right in the header. If you have neither of these, consider putting a sign-up button here to your email list.

Figure 14 – Ema Naito's site header contains site navigation with concise headings (including links in Japanese as this caters to her target audience), a search function top right and a clear description of what she offers.

Figure 15 – Siân Smith's minimalist header clearly states that she edits and proofreads non-fiction. It contains her logo, a search box, top-level navigation and links to her social media pages.

Footer

Your site footer appears on every page. It can help visitors who have scrolled to the bottom of your page without finding what they need (either because they've missed it, or it isn't there).

There is no definitive rule for footer content, but most users would expect the following:

- **Social media links and contact information** – Even if these feature higher up the page, include them again in the footer. People expect to see them here, and it makes it easier for folks to get in touch if this information is on every page.

- **Email sign-up** – If people are on a subpage that doesn't have your email sign-up button in the page body, they can easily access it here.

- **Copyright notice** – Your website content is protected by copyright law whether or not you include this notice, but it's always good to make it explicit. In your notice, show the copyright symbol, the year of publication (so always the current year) and your name. You can also include the word 'copyright' for clarity. For example: 'Copyright © 2026, Joanna Bloggs'. If your site includes content published over a range of years, include that, e.g. 'Copyright © 2020–2026, Joanna Bloggs'. Automate the current year to save you having to update it annually.

- **Website designer's name** – If you hired a professional designer to create your site, put their name in your footer (or they may have done this for you).

There are many other elements you can include, but be careful not to overcrowd the area. More ideas for footer content are:

- site navigation

- recent blog posts

- a photo of you and a short blurb about your services

- testimonials

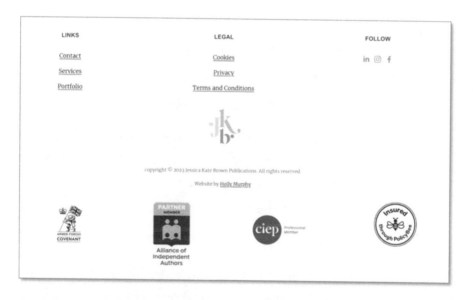

Figure 16 – Jessica Brown's footer has links to her top-level pages, 'small-print' content and social media presence. Below these sits copyright info and the name of the website designer. Jessica also uses this space to show her membership of professional organisations.

Calls to action

Calls to action (CTAs) are site elements (normally buttons, links) that require your visitors to act. When someone clicks on a CTA and signs up to your newsletter or follows a link to Amazon, this is known as a conversion. Think about your user journeys when designing and placing your CTAs.

To give your visitors the best chance of noticing your CTAs and clicking on them, try these tips:

- Use a contrasting colour to the background.

- Don't just include your CTA on the homepage; place it at multiple points throughout your site.

- Put the CTA in context for visitors to read any related content, so it makes sense for them to click.

- Make the CTA text clear and concise.

- Begin the link text with an action word, e.g. Sign up, Subscribe, Buy, Download. Don't just say 'More information' as it isn't engaging or descriptive of what will happen when they click.

- Use time-sensitive language, e.g. 'Sign up now'.

You can carry out A/B testing to experiment with changes to your calls to action. This is a great way to find out which colours, fonts and text lead to higher conversions. Remember to test just one change at a time, or you won't know which alteration is encouraging people to click.

Forms

The two main forms editors have on their sites are contact forms (for people to get in touch) and sign-up forms (for people to subscribe to a mailing list).

You may also choose to enrich your site by using forms for other purposes, e.g. a quiz.

Contact form

Keep this as short as possible and only ask for essential personal data, to comply with data protection laws and to encourage people to fill in the form.

A typical, effective layout is simply three fields:

- name (sometimes only first name)
- email address
- comment/enquiry, with the Submit button below.

Detailed pros and cons of using contact forms are covered in the 'Contact' section earlier in this chapter.

Sign-up form

This is for people to sign up to your email list, sometimes in exchange for a lead magnet (a freebie received upon subscription) and usually to receive a regular newsletter, blog updates and offers.

Your sign-up form should be short and only ask for essential personal data, for the same reasons as for contact forms.

As with all calls to action, the Submit button should stand out from the background. It should still be in keeping with the colour scheme of your site, but in contrast with its surroundings, so users have no doubt as to their next step.

Using first person from your visitor's viewpoint for the button text ('Sign me up', 'Claim my free guide') can also help to increase your conversion rate (number of people who click on the button).

Other tips for greater conversion:

- Test your form rigorously before releasing it. If a form fails to send, people won't come back later to fill it in.

- Feature social proof, such as a brief testimonial or review, next to your sign-up form.

- Tell them what will happen when they click Submit.

Reducing spam

If you're asking for people's email addresses via a form, you're opening yourself up to spam. This is impossible to completely prevent, but there are a couple of ways to drastically reduce it.

- **CAPTCHA** – This stands for 'Completely Automated Public Turing test to tell Computers and Humans Apart' (what a mouthful). It's an extra step on a form, where your visitor is asked to type in a series of letters or numbers that cannot be read by a spambot, to complete a simple game or to click on, for example, 'all the squares that contain a car'. These are effective at reducing spam but have a reputation for poor accessibility. However, since Google introduced an updated version, which can be negotiated with a single click ('I am not a robot'), the accessibility of these has substantially improved.

- **Honeypot** – This is a type of CAPTCHA that happens behind the scenes, so it doesn't interfere with user experience. It's a bit of code that people can't see on the page, but spambots (as they only read the code) can see and act on it. The spambot's email is not delivered, as it has revealed itself to not be human.

These techniques are easy to implement on many of the major website-creation platforms (e.g. WordPress), so take a look at the guidance offered by your web platform.

Accessibility of forms

Forms are notoriously inaccessible for people who use non-standard ways of browsing, for example, screen readers, mouse alternatives or keyboard-only browsing.

Take the following simple steps to improve the experience for users of alternative browsing methods, and by extension you will improve your site for all users.

- **Logical tabbing order** – This will help users of accessibility software, keyboard-only users and mobile users. Test your site by viewing your form on a desktop computer or laptop and tapping the Tab key a few times. You can also use a browser extension (e.g. taba11y for Chrome) to quickly visualise the tab order of elements on your webpages). If your cursor doesn't go from element to element in a logical order, you are giving users a bad experience. If using a WordPress theme, this may work fine automatically, but if yours isn't doing a good job, you can add a bit of simple HTML to ensure the tab order is right. Add `tabindex="x"` to each form field, replacing 'x' with a number to denote the tab order. For example: `<input type="text" id="name" tabindex="2">`.

- **Useful field labels** – Ensure your field labels ('Name', 'Email address', etc.) are crystal clear (in meaning and font!) and place them above your fields where possible, not in the box only to disappear when the user clicks. If you have good reason to have your labels inside the box, keep the text there until the user starts typing, rather than disappearing as soon as they click in the box.

- **Don't be too prescriptive for data inputs** – Be flexible with what data formats are accepted. For example, when asking for a date, ensure your form accepts 12/3/2026, 12/03/2026 and 12/3/26.

- **Helpful error validation** – If users incorrectly fill in a field, provide useful information as to what was wrong or what's expected, rather than just "Error".

Thank-you pages

If you have a unique thank-you page (i.e. a different thank-you page for each form on your site) that appears once they hit 'Send', you earn extra gold stars! This makes it easier for you to set up goals and conversions in analytics programs (e.g. Google Analytics).

8 – Images

Images can make or break a page. The higher the quality and the more relevant they are to your content, the more engaging they will be.

How do you feel when faced with a webpage full of text and not a single image? Overwhelmed? Disengaged? Bored?

Adding images will increase the time people spend on your site, and they can increase conversions.[10]

Size

There has been a definite shift over the past few years to larger images on webpages (in terms of dimensions, rather than file size). However, there is no one-size-fits-all rule, as it depends on the nature of the site and the message of the page.

---

[10] Peep Laja, 'How images can boost your conversion rate', *CXL*. 2022 (updated) [Online]. https://cxl.com/blog/how-images-can-boost-your-conversion-rate/ [Accessed: 11 March 2023]

Whatever the dimensions of your image, make sure it is as small a file size as possible to reduce page-load time.

Headshot

Include a professional headshot of yourself on your 'About' page and use the same image across all your media outlets (LinkedIn, Facebook, Instagram, conference websites, etc.). This will give a slick impression to your whole online presence and will help potential clients and fellow editors engage with you.

Stock or bespoke photos

There are many sources of copyright-free, cost-free images, but use these carefully. Cheesy stock images can make a visitor run before you have time to say 'Free download'.

Research has shown that using stock images on websites can reduce trust in a brand and the rate of conversions (newsletter sign-ups, clicks on purchase links, etc.).[11]

It can be tempting to fill your editor site with lots of stock photos of hands typing, people reading, or a pair of glasses lying askance

---

[11] Tommy Walker, 'Stock photos vs. real photos: Does it matter? Which ones work better?', *CXL*. 2022 [Online]. https://cxl.com/blog/stock-photography-vs-real-photos-cant-use/ [Accessed: 11 March 2023]

on a keyboard, but spending a bit of time coming up with an original idea will help your site stand out from the rest.

Try some of the following ideas to source unique images:

- **Get personal** – Rather than a stock photo of someone at any old desk or working on any old computer, source a decent image of you working at your desk, on your device. If you sell books on your site, get a photo of someone reading these.

- **Hire a professional** – Book a photographer for an hour to capture some images of you in different locations and poses (natural ones, not out of a catalogue). Let your personality shine through.

- **Plan well** – Make a list of the types of images that would engage you as a potential client, then hire someone (unless you know about professional-grade photography) for a short time to take those shots. Prepare well to make the most of the photographer's time.

- **Listen to advice** – Don't be afraid to ask for others' opinions. If you are hiring a photographer, tell them what you're aiming for (uniqueness, your personality/brand, variety for your site), and take their advice on board. You don't want to pay for a set of images that look like the stock ones you're trying to avoid.

I'm not saying you shouldn't use stock photos at all. If they are well chosen (not too cheesy or bland), well placed and mixed with bespoke ones, you may get away with it!

The eyes have it

If you're using an image of someone reading one of your books or resources, make sure they *are* reading it and not looking at the camera.

Figure 17 – Sunsilk study by Think Eye-Tracking showing heat map of users' attention on two versions of an advert.

Figure 17 shows the results of a famous eye-tracking study by Think Eye-Tracking, using a Sunsilk print ad. The red areas show where participants' eyes focused the most. There is far more interest in the product when the model is looking at it, rather than when she holds the gaze of the viewer.

Alt text and captions

Alt text is short for 'alternative text'. It is a text replacement of an image and doesn't visually show on the page unless the image doesn't display.

Captions display on the page, usually below the image, and are an enhancement.

Alt text

This is used when visitors can't see your image for a particular reason, including:

- visual impairment
- the link to the image is broken
- the browser or user has blocked the image for whatever reason

People with a visual impairment use screen-reading software that reads out webpage content to them. The software will pick up the alt text from the code behind the scenes, so the person doesn't miss out on the image content.

Alternatively, if the image doesn't display (due to either a broken link or user choice), the alt text will appear on screen, again for the purpose of relaying what the user is missing.

Alt text is also used by search engines and can be good for SEO, which is another reason to get it right.

To check if you've written good alt text, cover the image with your hand and read the text. Does it convey the image content? Good alt text would run something like: "Josephine Bloggs sitting at a white desk, typing on her laptop", or "Josephine Bloggs sitting on a bench looking at the camera, smiling". Bad alt text would be: "Laptop" or "Woman".

Captions

These are written with the intention of appearing with the image and do not have to be used, unlike alt tags which are essential for the accessibility reasons already described.

A caption should be used if the content of the image isn't obvious, adding value to the image. Examples would be a list of names for a group photo or an explanation of a technical image.

Only add a caption if you feel your visitors will otherwise be left in the dark about what your image conveys.

9 – Text

If your text contains errors or is difficult to absorb, you will lose your audience's respect and trust, and suffer lower conversions.

Some text improvements will help optimise your site for search engines (move your pages higher up search results), others will guide your visitors more quickly to what they need, whether they're reading the pages visually or using a screen reader.

Headings

Keep headings short and meaningful, so if they appear in the site menu, they are easy for users to scan and don't take up valuable space in the navbar or on the page.

Make headings relevant to the page content. Search engines rate headings more highly than page content, so, for example, if you only edit romance, name your copyediting page 'Copyediting romance' or similar, rather than just 'Copyediting'. Your chances of being found will increase if people are looking specifically for a romance copyeditor.

Heading structure

Using subheadings is a great way to break up large chunks of text, but you need to go about it the right way.

Use heading markup

Don't manually resize and format (e.g. bold) your text. Depending on what platform you're using to edit your site, this is usually achieved by selecting the text that will be a heading and choosing the relevant heading size from a drop-down list.

The reasons for this include:

- Screen readers can make sense of your page structure.
- It reduces the risk of inconsistency across your site.
- If you decide to alter your site-wide heading styles in the future, they will all automatically update across your pages.

Use correct sizes

Heading 1 is the top level and is likely to be the page title. In some templates, it may be used for the site header, so your page title may be Heading 2. It should be clear in your template which is the first one you can use in your page body (Heading 2 or Heading 3).

Each heading level is a subheading of the previous number. So, your page structure may look similar to that in Figure 18.

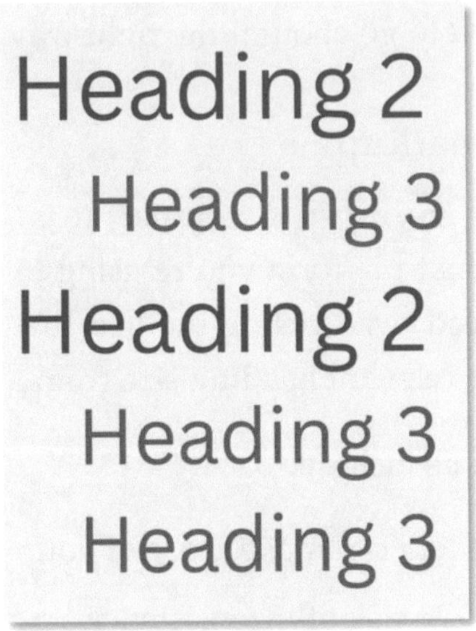

Heading 2
Heading 3
Heading 2
Heading 3
Heading 3

Figure 18 – Example of correct webpage heading structure.

Avoid missing out a level (jumping from Heading 2 to Heading 4, for example). It may be tempting to do this for design reasons (maybe you aren't keen on the look of Heading 3), but it will make your page less accessible to screen readers as they may interpret the jump as missing content, and your users will find it hard to understand your page structure. It's far better to alter your template and CSS (behind-the-scenes style code).

Copy

Repeated usability studies have shown that people read on-screen text more quickly than the printed page, scanning it rather than settling down to a hearty read.[12]

You may be tempted to make your site content as beautiful as the prose that you edit, but unfortunately this won't cut it with your online audience. They are mostly coming to your site with a question, and they want the answer quickly. Your job is to satisfy that need, and if they notice other bits and pieces along the way, so much the better (your calls to action, another interesting blog post, your glowing testimonials, etc.).

F-shape scanning

Users tend to scan-read on screen in an F-shape.[13] They read the first line or two of the page (top horizontal line of the 'F'), then along the next line or two (second horizontal line) before moving vertically down the rest of the page, where they scan the first few words of each line (see Figure 19).

---

[12] Angela Gorden, 'Are you skimming or scanning right now?', *Medium*. 2017 [Online]. https://medium.com/evernote-design/are-you-skimming-or-scanning-right-now-21bd674804d0 [Accessed: 11 March 2023]

[13] Kara Pernice, 'F-shaped pattern of reading on the web: Misunderstood, but still relevant (even on mobile)', *Nielsen Norman Group*. 2017 [Online]. https://www.nngroup.com/articles/f-shaped-pattern-reading-web-content/ [Accessed: 11 March 2023]

Figure 19 – Eye-tracking study by the Nielsen Norman Group shows the F-shape made by web visitors as they scan page content.

Improve your text easily

There are easy ways to help users in this 'F' scanning habit. These will break up your text and draw attention to important points:

- Write concisely in short paragraphs.

- Give each point or idea its own paragraph.

- Use subheadings.

- Create bulleted lists whenever you are listing more than two items.

- Emphasise using bold (not italics as they are hard to read on screen).

- Put the most important information near the start of your sentences and paragraphs (there's no need to create suspense!).

- Avoid jargon and ambiguous terminology.

Fix errors

Proofread your whole site, checking for typos, spelling errors, grammatical mistakes and missing words. This will boost your credibility as an editor and help search engines find your content.

Don't forget to check headings, links and buttons too, as these are often overlooked during the proofing stage.

If you feel you're so close to the content that you're becoming blind to errors, ask a friend to check it or hire a fellow professional proofreader. (Shameless plug: I specialise in editing and proofreading web content.)

These checks are important for any site owner, but they are especially important for us editors! If you have content errors or layout issues on your site, this will damage your credibility as an editor, and people will be reluctant to hire you to check their content.

Formatting

Keeping your text simple in appearance will make it easier to scan-read and will also prevent users with certain visual impairments (e.g. dyslexia) from experiencing issues.

Here are some easy ways to achieve this:

Use bold text for emphasis

Use bold text (sparingly) to emphasise an idea, instead of italics or capitals. Both are difficult to read on screen, and a sentence all in capitals strikes an aggressive tone. IS THIS SLOWER TO READ THAN THE PREVIOUS TEXT? CAN YOU TELL IF I'M SHOUTING, ANGRY, OR JUST WANT TO GET YOUR ATTENTION?

Use single spacing after full stops (periods)

Double spacing was used once upon a time to make the end of a sentence clearer when fonts were monospaced. Now that fonts are proportionally spaced, this is a superfluous practice that can create 'rivers' of blank space in the text for dyslexic readers.

Left-align text

Keep text left-aligned rather than making it justified (lining up the edges to the left and right, as in printed books). This will prevent uneven spacing between letters and words, which looks unsightly and also causes the 'river effect'.

Use sans-serif fonts

Sans-serif fonts can make paragraphs of text easier to read on screen and have a more friendly, open appearance.

Don't underline non-linked text

Don't underline text unless it is a link. Underlining will confuse visitors, who will try to click the text and assume the link isn't working.

Don't use black on white

Avoid using pure black text on a pure white background. This is too glaring and can cause issues for dyslexic readers.

Links

Links take the user to another place on your site (internal link) or to a page not on your site (external link). There are certain conventions to follow if you want your links to perform well.

Link text

Don't display the full URL (web address); use link text. This is the word or words that users click to go to another location.

Using 'human-readable' link text, rather than URLs, will ensure it's easy for your users to read, whether they can see the text or are using a screen reader.

Good link text tells the reader where they will go if they click, for example, 'Find out more about my services'. Avoid 'click here' because it's ambiguous, it doesn't apply to all devices (e.g. we tap on a mobile rather than click) and it's not accessible (screen readers pull up a list of all links on a page for the user to pick from, so 'click here' is not useful!)

Underline links

It's accepted best practice to underline links within the body of the page, rather than merely using a different colour, as people are used to this convention. Conversely, as already mentioned, don't underline text that isn't a link. Use bold instead if you need to emphasise something.

The traditional colour for links is blue (and underlined). While many designers have moved away from this, studies show that users still notice blue underlined links the most.[14]

---

[14] Matthew Woodward, 'How link color affects conversion – split test results', *Matthew Woodward.co.uk.* 2022 [Online].

Internal linking

Link to other pages within your site as much as possible. This will help your visitors to navigate your site, thereby removing dead ends. If you keep them moving from page to page, they will stay longer on your site, see more of your great content and find more calls to action.

What's more, the longer people stay on your site, the more important search engines will deem your content, pushing your pages up the search results.

Search engines also love internal links as they can easily crawl your pages to index them.

New tab for external links

A general rule of thumb for when a user clicks on a link is to make the new page open in the same tab if it is on your site, and a new tab if it is going to an external site. There are some good reasons for this:

- If an internal link opens in a new tab, it's confusing for a user, and it makes it harder for them to understand your site's navigation flow.

- An external link in a new tab will make it clear to users that they have left your site to go somewhere else.

---

https://www.matthewwoodward.co.uk/conversion/best-link-colors/ [Accessed: 11 March 2023]

- It will help your bounce rate (people coming to your site and leaving immediately without visiting a second page), as the original page on your site will still be open.

- A new tab for an external link will prevent your visitors from getting lost (they will be able to easily get back to your site as it will still be open on the original tab), or from having to keep hitting the back button to return to your site.

- Opening an external link in the same tab will produce inaccurate analytics, as it will show the user leaving earlier than they may intend to. They could be clicking on the external link (which will be recorded as a page exit if it opens in the same tab) before planning to return to your site.

10 – Social

You don't have to be on every social media platform. Concentrate on one or two, especially if you're starting out.

Is social media essential?

The short answer is No, but it helps. However, this comes with the caveat that if you aren't present on some of the big ones (e.g. Facebook, Instagram, LinkedIn), you should be working hard to build your email subscriber list. You will find it difficult to network with your audience and market your services through your website alone.

Social proof

This refers to how well you're regarded in the wider community. Testimonials, blog comments, Facebook shares and LinkedIn reposts are just some of the ways in which your social proof can expand.

Potential clients will take this into account, using the opinions of others to decide whether to hire you.

Reciprocal links

If you have a presence on LinkedIn, Facebook, Instagram and other platforms, provide links to these from your site through 'share' and 'follow' buttons, and from the social platforms back to your site. In fact, it's a good idea to provide links from each one to all the others, wherever possible, as this will consolidate your entire editor platform.

No matter which entry point is used by your audience, they should be able to access the whole shebang. This will improve your communication with potential clients and fellow editors.

Social meta tags

If you want control over what appears in your social media feed when you post a link to your site or when someone shares one of your webpages on social media, these tags are how to go about it. Without them, you have no control over what image (if any) displays, and what text shows.

There are two main types to concentrate on: Open Graph tags and Twitter cards.

You can either insert these directly into your code or add them using a plugin. If you're using WordPress, plugins that make this process easy include Yoast SEO and Jetpack.

Open Graph tags

Introduced by Facebook in 2010, these now influence content on other social platforms, including X and LinkedIn.

The most common Open Graph tags are:

- **og:title** – the title of your page or content as you'd like it to appear on a Facebook listing

- **og:site_name** – your site's name

- **og:description** – the short teaser text that displays in the Facebook post. Pay particular attention to this, as it is what will convince people to click.

- **og:type** – the category of content, e.g. blog, article, etc.

- **og:image** – the link to an image for your content, so that Facebook doesn't automatically display the first image on the page. Choose something that represents the content well and will pique people's interest. Images must be either PNG, JPEG or GIF format and at least 200px by 200px (ideally 1,200px by 630px).

- **og:url** –the URL associated with your content, i.e. the link.

Figure 20 – Example of how an Open Graph card displays in a Facebook feed. On the left is how it displays on mobile and on the right is a desktop view.

Twitter cards

X recognises both Open Graph tags and Twitter cards (yes, they're still called 'Twitter cards' at the time of writing, despite the company's rebrand to 'X'), but don't worry about a clash should you include both markup types in your site code. X will first look for a Twitter card. If this isn't present, it will use the Open Graph tags.

- **twitter:card** – the card type, which will be one of these: 'summary', 'summary_large_image', 'app', 'player'
- **twitter:site** –the @username of the business, used in the card footer
- **twitter:creator** – the @username of the content creator

- **twitter:title** – your page title

- **twitter:description** – short teaser text that displays in the tweet

- **twitter:image** – the link to an image for your content

Figure 21 – Example of how a Twitter card displays in a feed on X. On the left is how it displays on mobile and on the right is a desktop view.

11 – Search Engine Optimisation (SEO)

Optimising your site for search engines is a must if you want it to appear anywhere near the top of search listings.

Most web users don't get as far as Page 2 on a list of search engine results. Few people look past the top four or five results on Page 1. Do you?

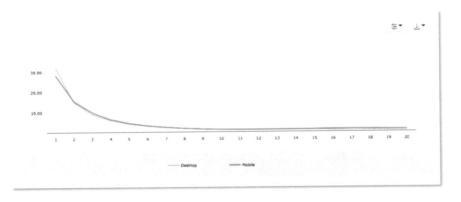

Figure 22 – Graph from Advanced Web Ranking, showing the sharp decline in click-through rate (CTR) after Page 1 of results, using statistics from August 2022.

There was a time when the description and keyword metadata in your site code were the main means by which Google (and other search engines) placed your page in search listings. If you ensured these were relevant, accurate and what people were searching on, your place amongst the top results was fairly assured.

Nowadays these two fields are not even considered by Google's algorithm.

While Google no longer uses the keyword and description fields to place your page, if you misuse these fields, it can count against you (for example, adding multiple instances of the same keyword).

The subject of SEO is vast and complex, not least because search engine algorithms are constantly changing. I've included here the main 'evergreen' ways you can make your site a friend to search engines.

'Behind-the-scenes' text for non-text elements

Your page content needs to be readable by search engine spider bots (bits of code that 'look' at your site to determine what it's about and what to do with it). They have the opposite appetite to human visitors – they like text, not images, videos and non-text content. Make sure your images have meaningful alt text (that accurately describes the image content) and any videos have good descriptions, ideally with captions or a transcription, or both.

All this 'behind-the-scenes' text serves double duty. Not only do search engines love it, but it also massively boosts the accessibility of your site, as screen readers (used by visitors with visual impairments) can only make sense of your content if text is included.

Relevant keywords in URL, headings and content

There may be endless keyword possibilities you could rank for, but your target audience won't enter all these when using a search engine.

Focusing on the keywords your audience is actively searching for will help your site attract visitors who will be interested in what you have to offer and who are more likely to convert to email sign-ups and enquiries about your services.

The first step is to work out the relevant keywords for your site. Think of your target audience. What search terms would they use to find your content? What problem or question do they have that you can solve for them?

Keywords to consider for your editor site are:

- your name

- your editing services (genre, topic, level of editing)

- your location (clients may prefer an editor based in the UK, for example, if they're writing in British English)

- types of English you work with (UK, US, Australian, Canadian, etc.)

See the next section – 'Fantastic content' – for more ideas.

Next, include these keywords in the content on the relevant pages. The higher up the page they appear, the more search engines will take note. So, if you can pinpoint a primary keyword or search term per page and ensure it is in the URL, title and first sentence of that page, this will do you a lot of SEO favours.

You can then put your secondary keywords through the rest of the page.

However, don't go overboard and flood your content with repeating keywords. This will make for a poor reading experience and may count against you.

Fantastic content

It's all very well getting people to your webpage, but if they don't like what they find, they'll quickly leave, and search engines will notice this. Google uses AI called RankBrain that notices dwell time (how long people stay on your page) and click-through rate (how many people click through to your page from search results).[15]

You need to answer a user's question or problem better than anyone else out there.

If you've had your editor website for a long time, it will be a little easier to get people to your site, as search engines will favour you in result listings because your domain authority will be higher. What do you do if your site is less well established?

Take a few minutes to ponder the following questions, then include the answers in your site content:

- How do your services help people?

- What do you offer that is unique? This may be related to your services, to you as a person, or both.

- What do more established editors who work on similar content to you include on their site that people may be searching for? (Be careful to only use their sites for inspiration; do not copy content under any circumstances. Not only is this highly unprofessional but also all online content is protected by copyright.)

---

[15] Sorav Jain, 'A complete guide to the RankBrain algorithm update', *ecoVME Digital*. 2022 [Online]. https://echovme.in/blog/complete-guide-to-google-rankbrain-algorithm-update/ [Accessed: 11 March 2023]

Clickable snippet content

This refers to the title, description and URL that appear in the search results entry for your page. If your site uses WordPress, the plugin Yoast SEO will help you to easily manage these fields.

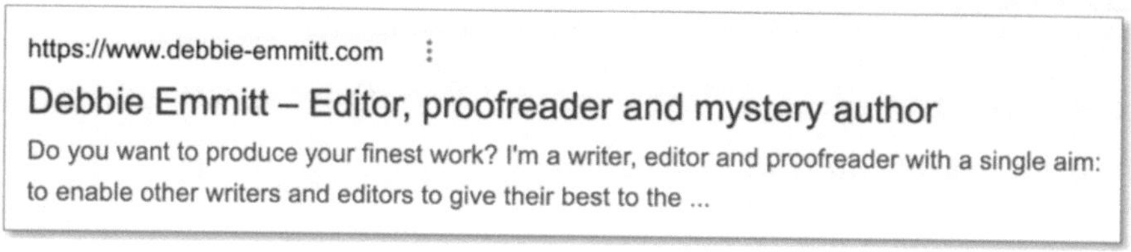

> https://www.debbie-emmitt.com ⋮
>
> **Debbie Emmitt – Editor, proofreader and mystery author**
>
> Do you want to produce your finest work? I'm a writer, editor and proofreader with a single aim: to enable other writers and editors to give their best to the ...

Figure 23 – How your webpage will look in a list of search results

There are some quick and easy steps for writing clickable page titles and descriptions:

1. Enter a search term people may use to find your site, then look at the Google Ads or sponsored search results. These are the promoted boxes at the top of the page. It can take a few attempts to see ads, as they aren't always available for your search terms.

2. Notice what words they use in their page titles and descriptions. As people are paying for these spots (and the only reason they're paying is to get clicks to their site), the ads you see are probably the winning results of testing and therefore stand the best chance for that site to get clicks. If there aren't any Google Ads or sponsored links showing, look at the top search results.

3. Use similar words in your page titles and meta descriptions, but be careful not to directly copy the content and ensure the keywords are relevant to your site.

Links

There are three types of links you need to know about: inbound, outbound and internal.

Inbound links (external sites linking to you)

These are also known as 'backlinks', and the important consideration is 'quality'. In essence, a quality site is one that ranks well in Google search results. Steve Napier, SEO consultant, has provided an extensive list of characteristics of a quality site.[16] You can also use this list to increase the quality, and therefore page ranking, of your own site.

The higher a site's quality (and the higher it ranks in Google), the better it is for you to have a link from it to your site. However, first bear in mind whether it is a relevant link. Don't just reach out to the top dogs because they are the top dogs.

---

[16] Steve Napier, 'What makes a website a high quality website?', *SEO Expert* [Online]. https://www.seomark.co.uk/high-quality-websites/ [Accessed: 11 March 2023]

There are a few ways you can increase the number of quality inbound links:

- **Be a guest blogger** – Politely approach the owners of blogs where your target audience hangs out and offer to write a guest post. Make sure a link back to your site is included.

- **Go on podcasts** – You can announce your web address on the episode, and it can also be featured in the episode blurb on your host's site and/or in the show notes.

- **Link to other sites from your pages** – This is easier if you blog as you're constantly creating fresh content from which to link to quality external sites. You don't need permission to link to another site, but it is polite to let them know you have done so. They may link back to you if there is a place on their site that is relevant.

- **Get active on social media** – Include your web address on your social profiles. While a link from Facebook or LinkedIn is not counted as a high-quality link as you are posting it yourself, it creates traffic to your site, which helps your SEO.

- **Comment (usefully!) on relevant blog posts** – When you do this, include a link to your site. Make sure the link doesn't come across as shameless marketing, but as a genuinely useful link that is pertinent to the blog post and/or your comment.

Ensure the inbound link is pointing to a quality page on your site that includes internal links. If people arrive there only to bounce straight out again, this will potentially have a negative impact on your SEO and undo the good work of the inbound link.

Outbound links (from your site to external sites)

It may seem counter-intuitive that these can help your SEO because people are leaving your site. However, outbound links, especially those of high quality (there's that word again) can have a positive effect on your SEO.[17]

Here are some tips when using outbound links:

- If you have a blog, link out to relevant webpages one to three times per post. Make sure the site you're linking to is of high quality and the content is useful to people reading your blog posts. The external content will ideally expand on ideas you have touched on but haven't covered in detail. This will be of value to your visitors, who will return to your post as the authority on that subject.

- Moderate all comments on your posts before publishing them. This will ensure that low-quality or spam links do not get auto-posted to your site and negatively impact

---

[17] Winnie Wong, 'Do outbound links matter for SEO in 2022? *SEOPressor*. 2022 (updated) [Online]. https://seopressor.com/blog/do-outbound-links-matter-for-seo/ [Accessed: 11 March 2023]

your SEO. Incidentally, a healthy level of interaction on your blog posts is another small boost for your search ranking!

- Force outbound links to open in a new tab, so if your visitors close that tab, they keep your site open. Simply add `target="blank"` to the end of the link in the HTML (code) or tick the box 'open in new tab' when creating the link in your content management system (CMS).

- Some outbound links can potentially harm your SEO, for example, affiliate links. Tell search engines to ignore these links by using the 'nofollow' attribute on the link. Either add it to the HTML if you know how to do this or toggle the relevant option in your CMS (WordPress has this function built in).

Internal links (between pages on your own site)

These are good for SEO because they help to make your site 'sticky' – that is, to keep people on your site.[18]

This is probably the easiest link tip to implement, as you (hopefully!) know the content on your site and can easily pinpoint places where you can add internal links.

---

[18] Yauhen Khutarniuk, 'Internal links for SEO: best practices for 2023', *SEO PowerSuite*. 2023 [Online]. https://www.link-assistant.com/news/internal-linking-strategies.html [Accessed: 11 March 2023]

Optimise pages for all devices, especially mobile

This will keep visitors coming back, make them stay longer on your site and encourage them to look at more pages, thereby telling search engines your site is the one people want to access.

Google unveiled its revised indexing system, mobile-first indexing, in March 2018, and in July 2022 it completed its switch to mobile-first for all websites.[19] This means that if your site doesn't work properly on mobile, it will affect your SEO.

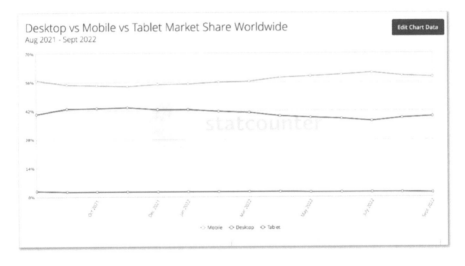

Figure 24 – Graph from StatCounter, showing how mobile usage is significantly greater than desktop.

---

[19] 'Google's mobile algorithm will be in place as of July 2022: Are you prepared?', *RAWWW*. 2022 [Online] https://rawww.com/googles-mobile-algorithm/ [Accessed: 11 March 2023]

To ensure your site doesn't lose SEO points as far as mobile is concerned, follow this advice:

Have one, mobile-friendly, version of your site

If your site has a separate, legacy mobile version, remove it and instead make sure your desktop (default) version is responsive (will display well on different-sized screens, including mobile).

Avoid 'read more' drop-downs

Don't hide content behind a 'read more' drop-down to make your content shorter for mobile users. Search engine spider bots can't access this hidden content. If they can't get to your content, they can't index it.

Be 'mobile-first'

Employ a mobile-first attitude to your site. Design for mobile primarily, not as an afterthought. You can check your site for mobile friendliness using Google's mobile-checking tool at: search.google.com/test/mobile-friendly

Frequent updates and fresh content

Exactly how much difference this makes to SEO is hotly debated. Search engine spiders are constantly trawling the web for new pages to index, so when there are new ones, or updated ones on your site, it helps to get your site in search results. However, it is only a small factor amongst all the other SEO advice here.

It goes without saying that an out-of-date site will not be popular amongst users, therefore will not generate many visits and/or will have a high bounce rate (people visiting one page and quickly leaving), which will have a negative SEO impact. However, it depends on your site content.

If you don't have a blog to go stale, don't have a news and events page to stagnate, and your content is fairly static, then not changing your site regularly will not make much difference to your search ranking.

It's far more important to focus on providing quality content and links than worrying if you have published new content in the last two months (unless you have a blog or news and events section, in which case, keep the fresh content flowing!).

Page description meta tag

This lives in the <head> of your site (in the behind-the-scenes code) and does not display on your webpage. Non-human users of your site (e.g. search engines, social media apps, browsers) use it to display your content as best they can in listings.

While it's no longer worth using the keyword tag, the description tag is still useful. Although search engines no longer rely on it to determine what your page is about (their spider bots can access all the text on your page to do this), a quality description of each page on your site has a small positive impact on your page ranking, and the text can be displayed in search results.

Small warning: Don't provide the complete answer to a user's question in your page description. They need to click through to your site to help your search engine ranking, so if you offer total satisfaction in your text snippet, they'll have no need to click through. This is one reason people are concerned about Google's plans to use generative AI. It will create summaries of information based on existing website data, so users may not be motivated to click through to the original webpage.

If you use WordPress for your site, there are plugins that can help you to easily add page descriptions. The most popular one at the time of writing is Yoast SEO.

Other considerations

There are lots of other small things you can do to improve your site's SEO, including making sure your content is well laid out, easy to navigate and written with the user in mind. In short, put into practice all the advice in this guide! This will entice people to stay longer on your site and keep coming back for more – activity that is noticed by search-engine algorithms.

12 – Site Performance

If your site is slow to load and doesn't work on popular devices, people will quickly leave and not come back.

Master the elements in this section, and you'll have a site that is a pleasure to use, no matter how people are choosing to access it.

Page speed

How long do you wait for a webpage to load before giving up? Five seconds? Four?

According to Google, the benchmark load time is three seconds.[20] This is a key length of time before dropouts happen quite dramatically.

---

[20] Matt G Southern, 'Google: new industry benchmarks for mobile page speed', *Search Engine Journal*. 2017 [Online]. https://www.searchenginejournal.com/google-new-industry-benchmarks-mobile-page-speed/ [Accessed: 11 March 2023]

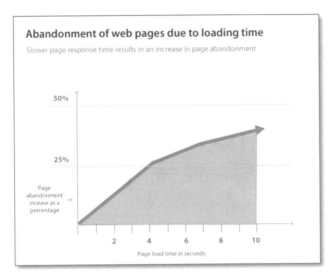

Figure 25 – This graph from Quick Sprout clearly shows how page-load speed affects page-abandonment rates.

The length of time a webpage takes to load depends on different factors, including:

- elements on the page, such as images and certain scripts

- speed of the user's internet connection

- number of visitors viewing the site at any one time

- caching settings (whether a previously loaded version of the page is saved, rather than having to call a fresh one each time).

Why is page speed important?

In a nutshell, slow load times can lose you visitors and, by extension, email sign-ups and potential clients.

In a 2016 study, the BBC found that, for every second of load time, they lost 10% of visitors.[21] A different study the same year showed DoubleClick by Google losing 53% of their mobile traffic if a page took more than three seconds to load.[22]

Given that mobile is now the preferred platform of users, this is a massive dent in site traffic.

How to check your page speed

There are lots of free online tools that will quickly check your site speed. Your site will need to be live for this to work, not under construction. Three examples of the many such tools available are:

- **Pingdom Website Speed Test** – You can choose one of several international locations from which to test, and the results are detailed but easy to understand, with recommendations on how to improve your page speed.

- **Google's PageSpeed Insights** – The results are not quite as accessible to less techy people and not as detailed as Pingdom, but it does give results for mobile and desktop, and recommendations for improvement.

---

[21] Matthew Clark, 'How the BBC builds websites that scale', *CreativeBloq*. 2018 [Online]. https://www.creativebloq.com/features/how-the-bbc-builds-websites-that-scale (Originally published in *.net* magazine in 2016) [Accessed: 11 March 2023]

[22] Matt G Southern, 'Google: new industry benchmarks for mobile page speed', *Search Engine Journal*. 2017 [Online]. https://www.searchenginejournal.com/google-new-industry-benchmarks-mobile-page-speed/ [Accessed: 11 March 2023]

- **WebPage Test** – Another detailed set of results that may take a bit of decoding. There is a handy summary of whether your site is quick, resilient and usable. You also get a pie chart showing you the elements of your page by size (byte) and requests to server. Recommendations on fixing aren't included in the report, but there is a link to help pages if you're happy to go searching.

A good approach if you have the time is to try all three tools, or find other tests that you get on with, then mix and match to get all the information you need.

How to improve your site speed

If you run your site through speed-checking tools such as those already mentioned, you'll be given advice on how to reduce page-load time. Some tips require technical knowledge, so if you have a developer, it's worth asking them.

However, there are some easy things you can do, even if you don't consider yourself technical. Remember, prioritise mobile page-load speeds, as that is the device of choice for most internet users and favoured by Google over desktop.

Reduce image size (resolution rather than display width)

There's no point having an image that is 3,000+ pixels wide, when the maximum size it will ever display on screen is 2,500 pixels or less. By reducing the size of your images, you will pick up some speed.

If you're not savvy with tools like Photoshop, a simple online photo editor such as Pixlr.com will satisfy your needs.

Most of the popular CMS provide plugins or native functionality that can automatically optimise your images to reduce their file size.

Reduce number of visual elements on a page

Each image and video is separately loaded onto the page by your visitors' browsers. If you have a lot of 'moving parts' on one page, they can have a significant impact on load time.

While it's great to include visual and audio-visual content, be aware of how much you're putting onto the same page. If you've written a 'how-to' blog post that includes many screenshots, make these as small (in terms of file size) as possible.

Change your hosting option

If your site attracts an extremely large flock of visitors and you are on a shared hosting package, you might want to consider moving to Virtual Private Server (VPS) hosting. This means that, rather than sharing resources with other sites, you have your own dedicated portion of these.

VPS hosting is more expensive than shared hosting, but you only need to consider this if you're generating heavy traffic. Contact your hosting provider to discuss if this would benefit you.

Remove unnecessary plugins

You may have plugins activated that you're no longer using. Do a bit of housekeeping on your plugin list. Be ruthless.

Removing unwanted plugins will have the added benefit of making your site more secure, as sites can be hacked via plugins that are out of date or that have vulnerabilities.

Paginate your blog post comments

If you're lucky enough to have lots of interaction on your blog posts, you may find it takes time for the page to load all those comments. Paginating them can help. If your site is on WordPress, this is easily done by going to Settings > Discussion and checking the box for 'Break comments into pages…' Other CMS will have similar functionality.

Add caching to your site

If you enable caching on your site, it can speed up page load.

The page will have to be visited once for the server to build a complete HTML file of your page (using all the elements of your page – images, videos, page text, any other code).

When the next person visits the page, they don't need to wait for the server to build the page from scratch again; they are simply served the cached version of the page.

If you then make changes to the page (so the cached version will be out of date), a properly set up caching system will detect the changes and rebuild the page the next time it is requested.

If you use WordPress, this can be easily done using plugins, e.g. WP Rocket (there are free and paid options, depending on how many bells and whistles you'd like). Use your favourite search engine to find the latest recommended ones. It's very easy to set up, and once done, can be left to run in the background.

Enable gzip compression on your site

Gzip compression is a way of making your website files smaller. Think of it in the same way as zipping up files on your computer. It may already be enabled on your site. To check, visit a free gzip compression checker – e.g. www.giftofspeed.com/gzip-test – and enter your web address.

If you find it isn't enabled, ask your developer to add code for this to the .htaccess file on your server, or if you're on WordPress, do it yourself via a plugin, e.g. WP Rocket.

This sounds complex, but it's a simple process and will make your users happier, as your pages will load faster (which all feeds into your SEO).

Accessibility

Web accessibility is often defined as ensuring a site can be used easily by someone with a disability. While this is certainly a key consideration, the concept is wider than that.

It is about making sure as many people as possible can access your site, regardless of disability, browser, device, platform or connection speed.

Different browsing experiences

There are lots of ways to browse that don't require a mouse, a conventional trackpad or even a keyboard.

It's a useful exercise to familiarise yourself with how all members of your audience access your site. You will see how having complicated content on your site, or visual content that isn't accompanied by text (e.g. alt text, closed captions) can drastically affect usability and severely hamper a user's experience of your site.

Take time to learn about some of the more commonly used alternative browsing methods.

Screen reader

A screen reader is used by people with a visual impairment. It is an automated voice that translates webpages into speech. It not only reads the on-screen text but also uses the code behind-the-scenes (HTML) to 'understand' and convey non-textual elements, e.g. links, images, tables.

You can easily hear how your webpages sound to someone using a screen reader by using one yourself. The two most popular free screen readers are:

- **NVDA (NonVisual Desktop Access)** – for Windows users. You can download it for free.

- **VoiceOver** – for Apple users. You can activate it by asking Siri to 'turn on Voiceover'. Alternatively, on an iPhone or iPad, turn it on in your Settings, or on a Mac keyboard, press Command-F5 (Option-Command-F5 to turn it off).

JAWS is the most popular screen reader,[23] although it isn't a free option and is designed for Windows.

Try to follow a user journey on your site using only the screen reader. You might be surprised to hear how people with visual impairments experience your site. If you come across a lot of issues, prioritise fixing those that completely block a user from completing a top task (e.g. subscribing to your email list, enquiring about your services, finding out more about you).

---

[23] 'Screen Reader User Survey #9 results', *WebAIM*. 2021 [Online].
https://webaim.org/projects/screenreadersurvey9/#used [Accessed: 11 March 2023]

Braille keyboard

This has eight keys that are used to form braille letters.

Screen magnifiers

The simplest of these, unsurprisingly, make webpage content larger, but the more sophisticated ones have other accessibility features built in too, such as glare reduction and contrast increase.

Sip and puff

This system is used by people with physical disabilities who are unable to control a keyboard, mouse or other browsing method. It consists of a straw that the user blows or sucks. These movements are then translated into keyboard commands or mouse clicks.

Hands-free cursor control

This category covers a range of systems, including FaceMouse (which interprets movements of the head into commands, a little like a joystick), LOMAK (the user points a head- or hand-mounted laser at the screen), and EyeGaze Edge (the user gives commands simply by looking at particular points on the screen – a webcam below the screen picks up their eye movement).

PCs and Macs have improved their native accessibility offerings in recent years. For example, macOS has the option of controlling your cursor with your head by using the built-in camera. You can set this up in Preferences > Accessibility.

Voice control

These systems allow users to give commands to their computer with their voice and incorporate speech-to-text capability. The most popular is Dragon.

Content management system (CMS)

Make things easy on yourself by choosing a CMS that supports accessibility. The most popular ones (e.g. WordPress, Drupal) certainly do, but it's best to check this for yourself.

Themes/templates

Just because your CMS supports accessibility, it doesn't mean that all the available themes/templates will be accessible. When you find a theme you like, check its documentation to see what it says about accessibility.

Things to consider

If you implement all the advice in previous chapters of this guide, your site should achieve a high level of accessibility.

In particular, if you get the following things right, you will have gone a long way to vastly improving the browsing experience of your site visitors with different physical challenges.

Use of colour

- Don't use colour alone to convey meaning. For example, if you have a sale price for a downloadable resource, don't rely on the colour red to denote this, but add text too, e.g. 'Sale price', 'Offer'.

- Use highly contrasting colours for text and backgrounds but avoid black on white as this can be too glaring and causes issues for dyslexic users. Try dark-grey text instead, or an off-white background.

Simple, concise content

Keeping your content simple will help every visitor to your site. People tend to scan-read online to find what they need, and shorter sentences written in plain English make this practice easier. It will also help people using magnification tools and screen readers, as there will be less text to plough through.

- Use short sentences and paragraphs.
- Break up text with subheadings and bulleted lists.
- Don't use a highbrow word when a simpler one is available.
- The 'Text' chapter (Chapter 9) has more information.

Correct heading structure

- Correctly mark up headings with tags (<h1>, <h2>, etc.).

- Use headings in the correct order (<h1> for the main page heading, <h2> for the next level of headings, <h3> for any subheadings below those), to ensure screen readers can make sense of your page structure.

- Don't pick a heading tag just because you like the look and feel of that heading style. Adjust your CSS to control the design, and stick to the correct order of heading tags.

- Don't skip a heading tag, e.g. from <h2> to <h4>, as this will confuse screen readers and may suggest missing content.

- The 'Headings' section in Chapter 9 has more information.

Image alt text

Alt text is what displays on screen if an image fails to load, or it is read out by a screen reader so that a user with visual impairment can make sense of the image.

- Add alt text to every image unless it's purely decorative.

- Use alt text that accurately describes the image content.

- The 'Images' chapter (Chapter 8) has more information.

Unique, descriptive link text

Link text is the wording on screen that is linked (usually a different colour and underlined).

- Avoid 'click here' as this doesn't tell your user where the link goes.

- Use link text that describes the destination, e.g. 'Link text tips in more detail'.

- Ensure each link has unique text, e.g. avoid multiple instances of 'Read more'.

- Put the most unique part of the link text first, to help screen-reader users who navigate by searching via the first letter, e.g. rather than 'More information about link text', use 'Link text tips in more detail'.

- The 'Links' section in Chapter 9 has more information.

Make forms accessible

Forms tend to be one of the least accessible areas of web content for people with disabilities. Often a task cannot be completed on a website due to a poorly designed form. All it takes is a bit of care when setting up the form, to avoid alienating a significant chunk of your audience:

- Label form fields appropriately so that screen readers can tell users what type of data goes where.

- Use a <label> tag on each field to clearly show what the field is for.

- Make sure the tab order of the fields is correct (if someone is using only a keyboard, not a mouse, they can tab through your form fields in the correct order, rather than jumping around or even missing out fields).

- Some CAPTCHAs (confirmation step on form submission to prevent spambots from sending form) are not accessible, e.g. those that only offer a blurry text image to decipher. This area is constantly changing as new CAPTCHAs are devised, so for the very latest advice, I'd recommend entering 'accessible captcha' into your favourite search engine and following the most recent advice given on reputable sites.

- The 'Forms' section in Chapter 7 has more information.

Tables for tabular data only, not layout

Screen readers read the code of the page, not what appears on screen. When they encounter a table, they will tell the reader that there is a table with so many rows and columns, then will read the table content in a set order.

- Only use tables when the information would be most clearly conveyed in rows and columns (tabular data).

- Don't use tables purely to fix your page layout; use templates and CSS instead. If you have used a table for layout purposes, the screen reader may not read the text in the order you intended, and the user will get lost.

- Use headers for rows and columns to explain the relationships of cells.

Content accessible with keyboard-only controls

Some users who have mobility disabilities may not be able to use a mouse or trackpad. Some will rely solely on their keyboard and navigate using the tab, arrow and Enter keys. Others may use an alternative input device, such as a single-switch input or mouth stick.

- Check the tab/arrow order of your content matches the visual order, so users can logically travel through it.
- Use anchor links to help page navigation.
- Ensure menus are accessible with keyboard controls.

Accessible dynamic content

Dynamic content refers to elements of your site that are more 'fancy' than the basic text, images and links. This includes items such as pop-ups, videos, modal boxes, screen overlays and more.

Depending on how users are browsing your site, they may not even be aware that something new has happened on the screen, for example, if they are zoomed in to a different part of the screen, or if they can't see the screen.

Follow these tips to help make your dynamic content accessible:

- Don't overuse dynamic elements.

- Use closed captions and transcripts for videos.

- Don't let videos play automatically when a page loads.

- Avoid flickering, flashing effects in videos and other animated content. This can trigger seizures in some users and can make others feel dizzy or sick.

- Slideshows and galleries should be navigable using the keyboard, and all images should have alt text.

- Make dynamic content accessible by using ARIA (Accessible Rich Internet Applications) markup text, e.g. by adding the role of 'alert' to a piece of alert text. Depending on how the alert is set up on your site, this markup text will be implemented in different ways, so it's best to research the type of alert (or other dynamic content) that is on your site … or ask a friendly web developer!

Responsive design

Responsive design is an aspect of accessibility. It refers to making sure your site functions and looks good in/on as many browsers, platforms and devices as possible.

I've put it in its own section because it's such a big deal and spans other areas too, such as SEO (although we could argue that many elements of SEO are there to make sites accessible, so all this stuff goes hand in glove!)

A quick reminder of terminology before we go any further:

- **Browser** – the application you use to look at webpages, e.g. Google Chrome, Apple Safari, Mozilla Firefox, Microsoft Edge
- **Platform** – this has a wide definition, but for our purposes in this section it refers to the operating system used to access the internet, e.g. Linux, Microsoft Windows, macOS/iOS (Apple), Android
- **Device** – the physical equipment used to access webpages, e.g. desktop/laptop, tablet, mobile

Mobile-first

If you take nothing else away from this section, remember one point: **Ensure your site works correctly on mobile.**

Why? Here are two massive reasons, amongst lots of little ones:

- Mobile phones generated 60.66% of website traffic in 2022, increasing by 5% over one year.[24]

---

[24] Christo Petrov, '51 mobile vs. desktop usage statistics for 2023', *Techjury*. 2023 [Online]. Available: https://techjury.net/blog/mobile-vs-desktop-usage/ [Accessed: 11 March 2023]

- Google uses any mobile version of a site as the primary version, so your desktop one will not get a look in. Far better to ditch the separate mobile version (if you have one) and have one version that is fully responsive.

You can check whether your site is mobile-friendly in just a few seconds by entering your URL on the Google mobile test page:

search.google.com/test/mobile-friendly

If it says your site is mobile-friendly, congratulations! However, it isn't the end of the road, as pages may still not be displaying 100% correctly. Nothing beats basic usability testing – check your site on your mobile.

There are also some great websites you can use to check how your site looks on all sorts of devices, including different makes and models of phones. Don't sign up or pay for this functionality; there are lots of sites offering this for free. Just look for 'responsive website checker' using your favourite search engine. Most browsers also have plugins you can use for the same exercise.

Know what your audiences are using

If you're tracking your site traffic, e.g. using Google Analytics, it's easy to find out the main browsers, devices and platforms that your visitors are using to access your site. These are the ones you need to concentrate on and ensure your site works with.

To find them in Google Analytics (GA4):

1. In the menu, go to Reports > Tech (under User subheading) > Tech details.

2. You will see a list of browsers like in Figure 26.

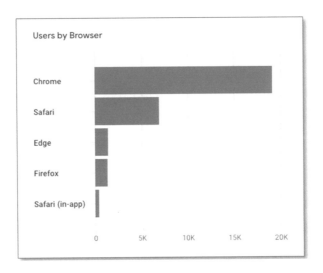

Figure 26 – List of browsers in Google Analytics

3. Scroll down to the table below the graph for more information. If you click on the dropdown in the first column's header, you can choose to see data about users' operating systems, device models and more.

4. On the Tech overview, you can also see the operating system people are using (Windows, Mac, etc.) to access your site and a breakdown by device (desktop (this includes laptop), mobile, tablet).

This is juicy information you can use to improve your site, as you can narrow down the browsers and devices on which to concentrate your testing.

There are online tools to check your site across different browsers and devices. Some of these are free, others offer a free trial after which you pay. Search for 'cross-browser testing' to find one you like.

Broken links

These are incredibly frustrating for a user. You will know from personal experience how annoying it is when a link promises the exact thing you've been looking for, but when you click on it, a message appears along the lines of, "Sorry, the page you're looking for cannot be found." Grrr.

Broken links are also known as 404 errors, as that is the response code returned when a browser connects to the server and can't find the specific page requested.

Why do 404s happen?

These can occur for a few reasons, including:

- the webpage has been deleted
- misspelled URLs on the actual site (and users are spelling them correctly)

- user error – mistyped URL in the browser bar

- incorrect referral link.

You can't prevent 404s being returned for the last two reasons, but you can do something to soften the blow, both for the user and for search engines, by using custom 404 error messages. More about these shortly.

You can easily fix the first two causes of broken links by setting up redirects.

Why are 404s a problem?

Firstly, user experience. If a visitor is already on your site, clicks on a link to another of your pages and encounters a 404, they will not be happy and may even leave your site. This could cost you a new client or an email sign-up and will impact your SEO.

If they arrive at a 404 due to a bad external link, they may never even see your site (although some users may be savvy enough to hack the URL in the browser bar back to your homepage or click on the logo in your header, which should be linked to your homepage). This will negate any positive search ranking you may have gained from that backlink, not to mention lost conversions.

Bad user experience aside, 404s can be damaging for your search ranking. If a user encounters a 404 from an external link, they are likely to hit Back very quickly in their browser. This tells Google your site didn't return anything useful for that keyword search and will demote you in search results.

Fixing broken links

If you delete a page from your site, be sure to add a 301 (permanent) redirect from the old URL to the new one. If you have knowledge of web code, you can add these redirects to the .htaccess file on your server. Alternatively, your CMS is likely to have a plugin to help you. I use a plugin called 'Redirection' on WordPress.

If there isn't a replacement page for the old one, redirect users to the next most useful page on your site, which may be the homepage or a page in the same section.

Don't merely redirect users to the homepage if this means they will be lost, or to a page that you'd like to get more traffic to, as this will be bad user experience and people will leave your site quickly, doing nothing for your SEO or conversions.

If you have misspelled the URL of a page that is already published, correct the typo and put in a redirect. People may have bookmarked the misspelled URL, so if you fix it without a redirect, they will get an error message.

Custom 404 pages

If a visitor mistypes the URL for a page on your site, or if an inbound link on an external site contains an error, you can't prevent a 404 page being presented. However, it's not all bad.

You can mitigate the damage, even improve your SEO, by creating a custom, branded 404 page that provides links to other pages on your site.

This will give people a better experience and they may stay on your site longer and discover more useful info than they otherwise would have done. You may even get a new client or sign-up out of it!

In case you need more convincing that custom 404 pages are friends to search engines, know that Google actively encourages you to create them.[25]

Make the content of your custom 404 page in keeping with the tone of your site. You could use imagery and language from your editing niche, or, if you're known for being witty, you could inject a bit of humour.

Use this tip with caution, though, as it can be annoying. We've all seen error pages that are trying to be funny or cool but don't quite pull it off!

---

[25] Google Console help pages, 'Create custom 404 pages', *Google.com*. [Online]. https://support.google.com/webmasters/answer/93641 [Accessed: 11 March 2023]

Some top tips for the content of your custom 404 page:

- Make it clear the page cannot be found.
- Include a search bar.
- Link to a few of your most popular blog posts.

How to check for broken links

There are free online tools you can use to check for internal 404s (links broken within your site), as long as your site isn't too large, otherwise it's a very slow process. Just search on 'broken link checker'.

If you have a large site, or if you'd rather not use an external tool, you can set up two custom reports in your analytics program, one for internal broken links, the other for external ones.

Depending on what you use (Google Analytics or something else), the method will vary. There are plenty of articles online about how to do this, so use your favourite search engine to find a step-by-step guide.

What to Do Next

Congratulations! You've made it to the end of this guide to improving your editor website.

You now have a solid grounding of knowledge to apply to your site. If you work on half, or even a quarter, of what you've learnt, your website and its position in search listings will be improved, and your visitors will easily find what they're looking for.

Leave a review

If you've found this guide useful, please consider leaving a review on Goodreads, StoryGraph and/or wherever you bought the book.

This will help fellow editors to find it and benefit from the advice too!

Learn more

Visit my website, which has more advice on managing your editor site: **www.debbie-emmitt.com/category/website-advice**

I'd love to hear from you if you have a question that isn't answered in this guide or on my site. If you have a query, you can guarantee someone else will have the same one, so please get in touch: **www.debbie-emmitt.com/contact**

Discover my mentoring service

My editor mentoring service will offer you advice and support on improving your online editor presence. It is carefully tailored to your requirements, no matter your level of expertise.

I will shape the sessions around your needs and goals for our time together, whether minutes, weeks or months.

www.debbie-emmitt.com/mentoring-for-editors

Stay in touch

Subscribe to my mailing list for a **free ebook** on the three most common writing errors, advice on the writing and editing life, language tips, and updates on my own writing journey straight into your inbox.

Find me on social media:

- **LinkedIn** – @debbie-emmitt
- **Facebook** – @debbieemmitt.editor
- **Instagram** – @debbie.emmitt.editor
- **X** – @debemmitt

Are you an author too?

Discover the other guide in my *Improve Your Website* series, for you or your author clients. It's packed with practical advice on every aspect of improving your author website.

Learn how to make an author site:

- Professional and appealing to readers and agents
- Appear higher in search results
- Accessible on multiple devices and platforms

www.debbie-emmitt.com/improve-your-author-website

Editors need editors

Are you looking for a trained, experienced editor or proofreader? I'm a Professional Member of the Chartered Institute of Editing and Proofreading (CIEP) and a Partner Member of the Alliance of Independent Authors (ALLi).

www.debbie-emmitt.com/editing-and-proofreading-services

About the Author

Debbie Emmitt is an editor, proofreader, mentor and author. With two decades of experience working with web content, she is passionate about sharing her web skills with the editing community.

She edits fiction, non-fiction and web content. Thanks to her degree in French and Portuguese from the University of Oxford and time spent living and working in France, she is particularly keen on editing books set in France.

Debbie is a Professional Member of the Chartered Institute of Editing and Proofreading (CIEP), a Partner Member of the

Alliance of Independent Authors (ALLi) and is working on her first novel, a mystery set in the south of France.

She lives in South Wales with her partner and two children.

Made in the USA
Columbia, SC
21 December 2023

29304156R00080